Praise for We M

"For all LGBTQ teens and young adults, this book will help inspire and empower you to become your best selves. This book shares how the LGBTQ community has made invaluable contributions. It throws open the doors of queer possibility making it clear we can use our imagination to make distinctive marks on our world however we choose."

—Dustin Lance Black
Academy Award-winning Screenwriter, "Milk"

"The need for positive role models in the LGBTQ Community has never been greater. In a divisive political climate, books like this one encourage and inspire LGBTQ youth to focus on their part in advancing society. Whether in science, technology, education, sports, government or the arts, the LGBTQ community has made an indelible mark on the world. Undaunted by prejudice, marginalization, discrimination and violence, the community has persisted and dedicated its efforts to the greater good. In the words of MLK Jr., "the arc of the moral universe is long, but it bends toward justice."

—Libby Schaaf
Mayor of Oakland

"When President Barack Obama came to our school system to highlight our early childhood programs, I had the privilege of representing Clairemont Elementary School. As a lifetime teacher, I so appreciate a book that shines a light on a previously marginalized community. We are an inclusive school system and this book can give us tools to expand the dialogue about history and change."

—Stephanie Trauner
Elementary School teacher for 26+ years, Clairemont Elementary School, a
Blue Ribbon school, City Schools of Decatur, Georgia

"Growing up in my Maori indigenous culture of New Zealand and with a father who was a leader of our local marae, sacred communal gathering place for 30+ years, I lived the value of community. We believe that we are never alone, our ancestors are always with us and so we share a collective an interconnected identity that helps us to stand strong in solidarity with our ancestors. This book may help you to remember that we are all connected to a global Rainbow family. Find our people - within family, friends, teachers, coaches, counselors, pastors who will support you and help you on your sexual orientation and gender identity journey. We are the potential of our ancestors, free and equal and we are never alone."

—Louisa Wall, Member of Parliament, New Zealand
Author of the Successful Marriage Amendment Act
Co-Chair of Cross-Party Rainbow Group, New Zealand Parliament
Co-Chair Commonwealth Women Parliamentarians, New Zealand Parliament

"Right now, more than ever, we need these stories of sheroes and heroes and gender-expansive warriors to inspire us on our paths toward justice. Kathleen and Eric have eloquently lifted up these stories for all of our benefit, showing us queer and trans people as powerful agents of change, love and liberation."

—Sean Dorsey
Trans Choreographer and Activist
Founder and Artistic Director, Fresh Meat Productions (2001-Present)

"We've had the audacity to fight for social justice for all LGBTQ citizens. This book is dedicated to all LGBTQ young adults and teenagers with big dreams and the perseverance to make those dreams come true. This book is sure to empower the next generation of LGBTQ youth to find their passions and transform the world."

—Kate Kendell, former Executive Director, National Center for Lesbian Rights

We Make
It Better

Also by These Authors

Eric Rosswood

The Ultimate Guide for Gay Dads: Everything You Need to Know About LGBTQ Parenting But Are (Mostly) Afraid to Ask

Journey to Same-Sex Parenthood: Firsthand Advice, Tips and Stories from Lesbian and Gay Couples

My Uncle's Wedding

Kathleen Archambeau

Pride & Joy: LGBTQ Artists, Icons and Everyday Heroes

"Seized," an essay in The Other Woman, edited by Victoria Zackheim

Climbing the Corporate Ladder in High Heels

We Make It Better

The LGBTQ Community and Their
Positive Contributions to Society

Eric Rosswood
and
Kathleen Archambeau

Mango Publishing

CORAL GABLES

Cover Design: Morgane Leoni
Layout & Design: Roberto Núñez

For permission requests, please contact the publisher at:
Mango Publishing Group
2850 Douglas Road, 2nd Floor
Coral Gables, FL 33134 USA
info@mango.bz

For special orders, quantity sales, course adoptions and corporate sales, please email the publisher at sales@mango.bz. For trade and wholesale sales, please contact Ingram Publisher Services at customer.service@ingramcontent.com or +1.800.509.4887.

We Make It Better: The LGBTQ Community and Their Positive Contributions to Society

Library of Congress Cataloging-in-Publication has been applied for.
ISBN: (print) 978-1-63353-820-7, (ebook) 978-1-63353-821-4
BISAC category code ########

Printed in the United States of America

Dedicated to all LGBTQ youth with big dreams. May this book help you reach your potential and find your place in the world. You are valid, you are loved, and you are part of something bigger. Together #WeMakeItBetter.

Table of Contents

INTRODUCTION

How LGBTQ People Make the World a Better Place

You probably learned about Martin Luther King Jr. in school. History books teach us that he was one of the most visible leaders in the civil rights movement, but did you know that Bayard Rustin, one of King's most trusted mentors and advisors, was an openly gay man? Rustin was instrumental in organizing the March on Washington, where King gave his famous "I Have a Dream" speech. Rustin also played an important role in the civil rights movement, but much of what he did was behind the scenes.

We've all learned about World War II in school as well, but did you know Alan Turing, another openly gay man, deciphered German codes that were significant in helping us win the war? LGBTQ people like Bayard Rustin and Alan Turing have played important roles in history. People in our community have made, and continue to make, significant contributions to the world. For example, Sally Ride was the first American woman in space, and was also the first known LGBTQ astronaut. Apple, the largest tech company in the world, is run by Tim Cook, an openly gay man. Under his leadership, Apple became the first publicly traded US company to hit a market value of one trillion dollars. When it comes to sports, Abby Wambach is an Olympic gold medalist who also holds the world record for international goals for both female and male soccer players. The Wachowskis are transgender siblings who directed *The Matrix*, which became one of the biggest blockbuster sci-fi movie franchises ever created, and Jóhanna Sigurðardóttir was the world's first openly gay head of government and Iceland's first female prime minister. That's right, we even run countries.

Did they teach you about any of these accomplishments in your school textbooks? Probably not. For some reason, there are people who have gone to great lengths to minimize or hide the accomplishments of LGBTQ people. Many of them have even taken it a step further.

Have you ever heard the phrase "No Promo Homo" before? It's a phrase used to describe laws that prohibit the "promotion of homosexuality" in schools. Some of these laws ban teachers from discussing LGBTQ people in a positive light, and some of them even require teachers to portray LGBTQ people in a negative way.

The UK had its own version of this type of law in Section 28 (or Clause 28) of the Local Government Act of 1988. The amendment stated that a local authority "shall not intentionally promote homosexuality or publish material with the intention of promoting homosexuality" and a local authority "shall not promote the teaching in any maintained school of the acceptability of homosexuality as a pretended family relationship." Section 28 was repealed in Scotland in 2000 and the rest of the UK in 2003, but these types of laws still exist in various countries around the world.

Russia has implemented a variety of provisions restricting expression, assembly, and funding, and support groups for LGBTQ youth are illegal because they are thought to promote "Non-Traditional Sexual Relations Among Minors." In the United States, where same-sex marriage is legal, there are still seven states (as of 2018) that have "No Promo Homo" laws: Alabama, Arizona, Louisiana, Mississippi, Oklahoma, South Carolina, and Texas. Alabama State Code § 16-40A-2(c)(8) states that classes should emphasize "in a factual manner and from a public health perspective, that homosexuality is not a lifestyle acceptable to the general public and that homosexual conduct is a criminal offense under the laws of the state." In South Carolina, Stat. § 59-32-30(5) mandates that health education in the state cannot include a discussion about "homosexual relationships except in the context of instruction concerning sexually transmitted diseases."

In addition to all of this, over half of the United States still allows conversion therapy, the harmful pseudoscience quackery that falsely claims to be able to change the sexual orientation, gender identity, or gender expression of LGBTQ people. The Williams Institute published a study in 2018 that revealed an "estimated twenty thousand LGBT youth in the US ages thirteen to seventeen will receive conversion therapy from a licensed health care professional before the age of eighteen" and "approximately fifty-seven thousand youth will undergo the treatment from a religious or spiritual advisor."

Why is it that some governments go out of their way to prevent people from talking about LGBTQ people, and in other cases, even try to convert us? People in the LGBTQ community have made positive contributions throughout history and we continue to improve society today. We set trends in fashion, film, music, art, and technology. We're Academy Award winners, Grammy Award winners, Pulitzer Prize winners, and Olympic gold medalists. We're doctors, lawyers, judges, politicians, and religious leaders. We run businesses, and we even run countries.

It is important to feature LGBTQ role models and highlight their contributions to society. Hopefully, these stories will inspire people around the world and help them realize that being LGBTQ is something to celebrate. Our community has made significant contributions to society, and that's something to be proud of. We're here, we're queer, and we make the world a better place. #WeMakeItBetter.

Part 1

ACTIVISM

Bayard Rustin

Civil Rights Activist

"People will never fight for your freedom if you have not given evidence that you are prepared to fight for it yourself."

Chances are you've heard of Martin Luther King Jr. and his famous "I Have a Dream" speech, but did you know Bayard Rustin, an openly gay man, was a mentor to King and instrumental in organizing the March on Washington, where that speech was given?

Rustin, who was no stranger to fighting for equal rights, traveled to India in the 1940s and studied the nonviolent resistance practices taught by Mahatma Gandhi. He combined those teachings with the pacifism of the Quaker religion and the socialism supported by African-American labor leader A. Philip Randolph to come up with his own approach to fighting for equal rights. In the 1950s, he met Dr. Martin Luther King Jr. and advised him on the tactics of nonviolent civil disobedience.

As a mentor to King, Rustin helped him organize the successful Montgomery bus boycott, which ultimately led to the Supreme Court ruling it unconstitutional for Alabama and Montgomery to legally require segregation on their public transit system. He remained a close advisor to King for the next few years.

In the 1960s, Rustin became the Deputy Director for the March on Washington for Jobs and Freedom. He was a key strategist for the march, and, with his team, created and distributed a manual, which included demands and a roadmap that helped transform American civil rights, labor rights, and education and housing policies. This policy agenda played a crucial role in helping to secure passage of the Civil Rights Act of 1963 and the Voting Rights Act of 1964.

Rustin was involved in numerous boycotts and protests throughout his life, always fighting to protect and advance the rights of minority groups. He died in 1987 and was survived by Walter Naegle, his partner of ten years.

In 2013, Rustin was selected as an honoree in the United States Department of Labor Hall of Honor. That same year, President Obama posthumously awarded him the Presidential Medal of Freedom, the highest civilian award in the United States. Even though Rustin was pushed behind the scenes because of his sexuality and political affiliations, he leaves behind a legacy that helped transform equal rights in the United States.

Emma González

Gun Control Activist

"There will always be people that hate you, and they're always going to be wrong."

O n Valentine's Day, February 14, 2018, a teenager shot and killed seventeen people at Marjory Stoneman Douglas High School in Parkland, Florida. It was one of the deadliest shootings in modern American history. The following day, the *Guardian* reported that there had been 1,624 mass shootings in the US in the 1,870 days prior. These senseless acts of violence had become commonplace in America, and little was done in response to them other than people offering their "thoughts and prayers" while waiting for the next one to occur. But this time was different. This time, the students relentlessly spoke up to push for gun safety laws, and one of those students was eighteen-year-old Emma González. Days after the shooting at her school, González gave a speech at a federal courthouse in which she put pressure on politicians and the NRA. Within moments, the speech went viral. Shortly after the rally, González and her classmates attended a town hall hosted by CNN, where they stood up to NRA spokesperson, Dana Loesch. González made such an impact at the event that her Twitter account quickly gained more followers than the official NRA account.

In less than a month after the shooting, the students pressured Florida politicians to take action, passing the "Marjory Stoneman Douglas High School Public Safety Act." The law raised the minimum age for buying a gun from eighteen to twenty-one, allocated money to mental health assistance in schools, established waiting periods and background checks, allowed for the arming of some teachers, banned bump stocks, and more. The students then went on to lead the March for Our Lives protest against gun violence, in which more than two million people participated in Washington, DC, and around the world.

González, who is openly bisexual and ran her school's Gay-Straight Alliance for three years, continues to work with her fellow students to push for meaningful gun legislation in the States and to prevent the reelection of politicians who take money from the NRA.

Nyle DiMarco

Model, Actor, and Activist

"With sign language, I was able to embrace my own identity as Deaf. I did not let being Deaf define me. Instead, I defined it."

Nyle DiMarco has been breaking down barriers and stereotypes ever since he was thrust into the spotlight when he appeared on the television show *America's Next Top Model* in 2015. DiMarco was the first deaf contestant in the history of the show. Since he uses American Sign Language with facial expressions and body movements, his deafness amplified his natural talent, helping him win the competition. Soon afterward, DiMarco broke down stereotypes again when he became a contestant on *Dancing with the Stars*. Even though he couldn't hear the music, being a visual person, he was able to pick up on small details and cues provided by his dance partner. And while he wasn't the first deaf person to compete on *Dancing with the Stars* (that credit goes to Marlee Matlin), he was the first deaf contestant to win on the show. Many people have the misconception that deaf people can't dance because they can't hear the music. By appearing on the show, DiMarco brought deaf culture into the households of millions of Americans and showed them that the only thing deaf people can't do is hear. Other than that, they can do anything else other people can do.

Winning television competitions has given DiMarco a giant platform to advocate and raise awareness for issues relating to the deaf community. He created the Nyle DiMarco Foundation, a 501(c)(3) non-profit organization dedicated to improving the lives of deaf people around the world, with a focus on bilingual education (American Sign Language and English) for deaf children. According to the World Federation of the Deaf, there are seventy million deaf people around the globe, and only about 2 percent of them have access to sign language education. When children do not have early access to language, they can have difficulties in functioning, socializing, communicating with other people, and overall learning. That's why, through his foundation, DiMarco has worked toward ensuring that all deaf children in the United States have access to language before they reach five years of age.

Taking his message global, DiMarco addressed the United Nations in 2018 and helped them mark September 23 as the first International Day of Sign Languages. During his visit, he raised awareness of sign languages and the rights of persons with disabilities all over the world. He also advocated for more countries to recognize sign language as an official language.

In addition to being an inspiration to millions of deaf people, DiMarco is also a role model for people in the LGBTQ community. *Attitude* magazine honored him with its 2017 Man of the Year award for being a tireless fighter for equality. DiMarco identifies as genderfluid and lives his life out and proud, encouraging everyone to embrace their own identity in order to thrive.

Cecelia Maria Zarbo Wambach, PhD

Humanitarian and Educator

Cecelia Wambach on the right.

"They all have PTSD. Many of them have seen their parents killed in front of them. The stories are heartbreaking and the kids are magnificent."

When Cecelia Wambach was growing up as the second-oldest child in a family of fourteen children in Pennsylvania, she never dreamed she'd be traveling to Lesbos, Greece, to help refugee children from Syria, Afghanistan, Sudan, and other war-torn countries. She's become an ambassador of compassion. Her bicultural Italian and Bohemian Jewish roots, along with a Catholic education, imbued Dr. Wambach with a calling to use her talents and gifts to create a better world. And the Jewish concept of *Tikkun Olam* spurred her desire to *heal the world*.

A PhD in Math Education from Fordham University led her, eventually, to San Francisco State University, where she started an urban education program in an inner-city school. While serving as both professor and co-principal of John Muir Elementary School, the Muir Alternative Teacher Education program she developed won the CCTC Quality of Education Award for Service to Teachers and Children.

Dr. Wambach, who has been married to her wife for over twenty years and is now a grandmother to four, retired as Professor Emerita. But her calling to help children was strong, and she soon found herself cultivating educational solutions for refugees "stuck" on the Greek Island of Lesbos, fewer than five miles from the Turkish coast. As the founder and Volunteer Director of Refugee Education and Learning International (REAL International), a 501(c)(3), Dr. Wambach brought all of her skills to bear in giving traumatized children creative educational experiences. She also fundraised for the organization, and recruited and trained volunteers.

Collaborating with the Greek non-government organization Together for Better Days, Dr. Wambach and the volunteers at

REAL International have worked to create learning centers for asylum-seeking refugees. They help unaccompanied minors and young adults displaced by war and extreme poverty to learn about topics such as computing, ecology, languages, and humanities.

According to UNICEF (United Nations International Children's Emergency Fund), only 29 percent of the twelve thousand school-age refugee and migrant children ages six to seventeen in Greece received formal education during the 2016–17 school year, and refugee and migrant children have missed an average of two and a half years of school due to conflict and displacement. Dr. Wambach hopes to improve those statistics. Back in the States, she actively recruits volunteers and accompanies them once or twice a year, for months at a time. The safe space of school allows refugees to explore, play, and learn and affords Dr. Wambach yet another opportunity to practice *Tikkun Olam, to repair the world.*

Part 2

BUSINESS

Beth Ford

President and CEO, Land O'Lakes

"The mission of agriculture is a noble one: do the work to feed the world."

B eth Ford is a living example of the American dream. She started small, worked hard, and climbed her way up the corporate ladder, becoming one of the top business executives in the United States. Ford was born in Iowa, and she has seven older brothers and sisters. Her first job as a teenager was de-tasseling corn and cutting out weeds in soybean fields for two dollars an hour. By age fifty-four, she was the first out lesbian CEO of a Fortune 500 company and just one of the twenty-five women CEOs in the same list. Ford got her undergraduate business degree from Iowa State University and her master's degree from Columbia University. She went on to hold senior-level positions at large organizations such as Mobil Corporation, PepsiCo, Scholastic, and Hachette before joining Land O'Lakes in 2011.

Land O'Lakes is a farmer-owned dairy and agriculture company with ten thousand employees working in fifty US states and fifty countries. They have a farm-to-fork view of agriculture, and are focused on the challenge of feeding more people while using less water and less land. During her tenure at Land O'Lakes, Ford was able to get the company to invest in technology and R&D, resulting in more plant-friendly farming techniques. She led them through record performance and growth, and helped the cooperative move beyond its reputation of just selling butter. When Land O'Lakes promoted Ford to CEO in 2018, she had helped the fourteen-billion-dollar co-op become one of the nation's largest food and agriculture cooperatives, ranking number 216 on the Fortune 500. The company's press release welcomed Ford to the new role and detailed her extensive experience. It ended by saying, "Ford and her spouse, Jill Schurtz, have three teenage children and live in Minneapolis." That statement made headlines around the world when people realized a company on the Fortune 500 would finally have an openly lesbian CEO.

In 2018, she was ranked number thirty on Fortune Magazine's "Most Powerful Women in Business List." At a time when a Human Rights Campaign survey has found that nearly half of all American LGBTQ workers are in the closet, Ford's rise is impressive. "I made a decision long ago to live an authentic life, and if my being named CEO helps others do the same, that's a wonderful moment."

Rick Welts

President and CEO, Golden State Warriors

*"I hope that my being here is some recognition
for all the people behind the scenes for the
sport of basketball that they love."*

S tarting his career in 1969 as a ball boy for the Seattle
SuperSonics, Rick Welts spent decades rising through
the ranks to become one of the NBA's top executives, and
eventually one of the most respected executives in the industry.
From 1982 to 1999, Welts worked at the NBA league office in
New York, and eventually became the Executive Vice President
and Chief Marketing Officer of NBA Properties. During
this time, he created the massively successful NBA All-Star
Weekend, in addition to the marketing program for the 1992
Olympics "Dream Team." When America's interest in the sport
soared, Welts was credited with enhancing the league's image
and making basketball the popular sport it is today.

One of his basketball legacies came about when he joined
sports attorney Val Ackerman to create the Women's National
Basketball Association (WNBA). The two were instrumental
in launching the women's professional basketball league
and securing partnerships with some of the biggest sports
advertisers in the world, including Nike, Coca-Cola, and
McDonald's. Together, for their efforts, he and Ackerman
were named BRANDWEEK's '97 Grand Marketers of the year.
Later, Welts became the President and Chief Executive Officer
of the Phoenix Suns, and they won three Division Titles (2005,
2006, and 2007) during his tenure with the team.

But one of his most meaningful moments was in 2011,
when he publicly came out in a front-page story in the *New
York Times*. By doing so, Welts became the first openly gay
executive of a major sports team, and an inspiration to many.
He received awards from GLAAD, GLSEN, and even served as
the celebrity Grand Marshal in the 2015 San Francisco Pride
Parade. He also became an Advisory Board Member for the
You Can Play Project, an organization dedicated to ensuring

the safety and inclusion of all people in sports, including LGBTQ athletes, coaches, and fans. Shortly after coming out, and weeks after leaving the Suns, Welts was recruited by the Golden State Warriors. During his time as President and Chief Operating Officer, the Warriors have excelled, winning three NBA Championships (2015, 2017, and 2018). Welts has had a remarkable career spanning over forty years, and in 2018, he was inducted into the Naismith Memorial Basketball Hall of Fame. In his acceptance speech, he acknowledged his lifelong love of sports and its power to bring people together. He also thanked his partner, Todd Gage, and said that, even though he has accomplished many things throughout his career, coming out was the most important thing he had ever done.

Suze Orman

Personal Financial Expert

"People first. Then money. Then things."

For fourteen years, every week, Suze Orman reached three million people with *The Suze Orman Show*, an Emmy Award-winning program about money and personal financial independence. She became America's go-to person for financial advice and, in addition to hosting her own show, made regular appearances on various others including *The View, Anderson Cooper 360, Good Morning America*, and *Larry King Live*. As the host of one of CNBC's most successful television shows, Orman would take calls from viewers and give them advice on how to fix their financial problems, discussing everything from paying off student loan debt to saving for a mortgage. She educated millions of people on stocks and bonds, and explained how long it would take to pay off their credit cards if they only made the minimum payment. Orman is known for tough love, telling it like it is, and never sugarcoating her message to viewers.

In addition to her television show, Orman is the author of nine consecutive *New York Times* bestsellers. Her books educate readers on how to be smart with money in any situation. She was a longtime contributing editor to *O, The Oprah Magazine* and a regular columnist for *AARP* magazine. She was included in *Forbe's* list of the World's 100 Most Power Women and was twice named to *Time* magazine's list of the World's 100 Most Influential People. While on top of the world, Orman came out in a 2007 interview with the *New York Times*. She said she was in a seven-year relationship with her life partner, K.T. The two were married in 2010 and have since retired to a mansion in the Bahamas. Her advice to you, no matter what your background or challenges are, is: "If you hold on to your goals and dreams, you will get there."

Tim Cook

CEO, Apple

"The sidelines are not where you want to live your life. The world needs you in the arena."

M any people know that Steve Jobs was the co-founder of Apple and the product visionary of the company, but did you know it was a gay man who turned their leading product, the iPhone, into one of the most successful tech products in history? Tim Cook became the CEO of Apple in 2011, and, three years later, became the first openly gay man to run a Fortune 500 company, after coming out of the closet in a *Bloomberg* editorial. As if that wasn't enough, Apple became the first one-trillion-dollar publicly traded US company under his leadership.

Most of Apple's profits have been driven by the iPhone, which tens of millions of Americans use in their everyday lives to make calls, send texts, take pictures, check email, listen to music, post on social media, play games, and more. Cook used the product to take high-tech security features normally only used by businesses and made them available to homes around the world. Ordinary people suddenly had the capability of unlocking their devices using fingerprint technology or by scanning their faces, something that was previously only seen in sci-fi movies. He also revolutionized the way consumers make purchases when Apple rolled out a digital wallet, giving people the ability to replace their credit cards with their phones when making in-person purchases.

In addition to being a leader in the business and technology fields, Cook is also a leader when it comes to social issues, and has a long history of supporting LGBTQ equality. In 2013, he wrote an opinion piece in the *Wall Street Journal*, urging the US Senate to pass the Employment Non-Discrimination Act (ENDA), a bill that would ban employment discrimination based on sexual orientation and/or gender identity. In 2015, he pushed even harder for LGBTQ equality. He wrote an op-ed in the *Washington Post* against "religious freedom" bills (laws that would legalize discrimination against LGBTQ people if done for religious reasons), wrote a statement to the Human Rights Campaign in support of the Equality Act (a bill that would provide protections from discrimination for LGBTQ people in employment, housing, credit, education, and other key areas of life), and he even got Apple to file a joint friend-of-the-court brief to the US Supreme Court, urging them to overturn same-sex marriage bans. When the court finally ruled that marriage equality was legal across the country, Cook celebrated by marching in the San Francisco Pride Parade with approximately eight thousand Apple employees.

Cook has also used his platform, and Apple's position of influence in the world, to stand up on other social issues, such as racism, immigration, and climate change. For example, after the 2017 alt-right rally in Charlottesville, Virginia, that left one counterprotester dead and nineteen people injured, Cook pledged one million dollars in donations to both the Southern Poverty Law Center and the Anti-Defamation League. In 2017, Apple joined other companies in filing a joint court brief against Trump's stringent Executive Order on Immigration, which halted entry of all refugees and banned citizens from seven predominantly Muslim nations. The companies all agreed that increased background checks were important, but so was America's commitment to welcoming immigrants. The brief made the claim that "Immigrants do not take jobs away from US citizens—they create them," while pointing out that immigrants or their children founded more than two hundred of the Fortune 500 companies, including Apple. In his role as CEO of the largest tech company in the world, Tim Cook has proved that LGBTQ people can be great business leaders. Ironically, even more than his stellar leadership, big heart, and generous financial contributions, Cook's forthright example as the most recognizable gay person in the public eye is likely to have the most far-reaching impact on all youth, both queer and straight.

Part 3

DANCE

Bill T. Jones

Dancer and Tony Award–Winning Choreographer

"We can get up and do it over again, better."

When it comes to modern dance, Bill T. Jones is one of the most notable choreographers and directors of our time. He was born the tenth of twelve children to migrant potato pickers and studied at Binghamton University, which he attended on a special program for underprivileged students. While there, he studied West African and Afro-Caribbean dance, classical ballet, and modern dance. From there, he went on to become the Artistic Director of New York Live Arts and Artistic Director/Co-Founder of the Bill T. Jones/Arnie Zane Dance Company.

Politics, race, and social issues have often been themes in Jones' work. As a longtime AIDS survivor, HIV and AIDS have frequently been highlighted in his pieces. He choreographed *Absence*, which showcased heartrending performances that expressed his grief following the death of his partner, Arnie Zane, who died of AIDS-related lymphoma. In 1994, he choreographed *Still/Here*, a controversial piece that explored mortality and what it's like to live with a life-threatening medical diagnosis. His work gained national attention, and in that year, he graced the cover of *Time* magazine.

Jones also made a significant mark on the Broadway stage. In 2007, he won the Tony Award for Best Choreography for the musical, *Spring Awakening*, the story of a nineteenth-century German schoolgirl coming of age and the collective rebellion of German teens in an era of repression and structure. In 2010, he again won the Tony Award for Best Choreography, this time for *FELA!*, a musical based on the life of Fela Kuti, the Afrobeat musician and activist who was jailed numerous times in his young life and was severely beaten after speaking out against the Nigerian army. Jones has received prestigious honors for his provocative work that spans decades. He was inducted into the American Academy of Arts and Sciences in 2009, and was a Kennedy Center Honoree in 2010. He was recognized as Officier de l'Ordre des Arts et des Lettres by the French government, and was even chosen for the National Medal of Arts by President Obama in 2013. When it comes to performance arts, Bill T. Jones has definitely left his mark.

Jin Xing

Award-Winning Dancer, Talk Show Host, and Entertainer

"I don't want to change the world, but I also don't want the world to change me too much. I just want to be myself."

An army colonel and a prima ballerina may seem like polar opposites, but both of them adequately describe Jin Xing. Born in Shenyang, Liaoning, China, in 1967, Xing joined the People's Liberation Army performance troupe when she was only nine years old. In the military, she spent part of her time studying dance and performance arts while, at other times, learning how to use bombs, grenades, and machine guns. Though the two disciplines don't seem to go together, Xing credits much of her success in her professional life to the military discipline she learned while serving in the army. Xing won her first national dance competition at age seventeen and became one of the most celebrated dancers in China. This led her to apply for, and win, a scholarship to study modern dance in America. After critical acclaim in the States, she performed all over Europe before returning home to China.

Her time spent traveling the world gave her the opportunity to reflect on who she was as a person. From an early age, Xing knew she was female, and at age twenty-eight, she decided it was finally time to transition. Since China is such a conservative country, it was risky to be one of the first citizens to have gender confirmation surgery. Acceptance was slow at first, but society eventually embraced Xing. She was the first transgender person to be officially recognized by the Chinese government, and has since been able to adopt three children and get married.

In addition, she has risen to become one of China's most popular entertainment personalities. Along with forming the Beijing Modern Dance Company and the Jin Xing Dance Theater, Xing became a popular judge on the local version of *So You Think You Can Dance*. Audiences loved her so much that she wound up getting the opportunity to host some of

China's most popular TV shows, including her own variety/ chat program called *The Jin Xing Show*, which had an estimated one hundred million viewers every week, and a show called *Chinese Dating with the Parents*, where parents decide who their sons can date. While the latter may sound a bit controversial, Xing says the show depicts real life in China, where parents still play a major role in whom their children marry. Xing has done many things in her life. She's been a military colonel, a choreographer, a prima ballerina, a competition judge, a television host, and more, but one thing has always remained consistent. Xing commands attention and stands out in a crowd. Above all, she's an entertainer.

Part 4

FILM & TELEVISION

Daniela Vega

Award-Winning Actress

"Soy muy auténtica." ("I'm the real deal.")

Born in Santiago in 1989, Chilean native Daniela Vega found it difficult to find work after transitioning. So much so that she started getting depressed. But everything started looking up when someone she knew asked her to be part of a makeup team for a theater production, marking the beginning of Vega's journey to success. Through a friend, Vega began sitting in on courses at university. She sang and tried out for stage roles, further developing her love of the performing arts. Eventually, she acted in a solo show about her transition, *La Mujer Mariposa* (*The Butterfly Woman*), which ran for eight years in Santiago. After her screen debut in the 2015 Chilean film *La Visita*, Vega ultimately landed the role of a lifetime.

Director Sebastián Lelio initially approached Vega to be a culture consultant for his film, *Una Mujer Fantástica*, (*A Fantastic Woman*), but after working with her for a while, he felt she would be perfect for the starring role. It's common to cast cisgender actors in transgender roles (Jeffrey Tambor in *Transparent*, Felicity Huffman in *Transamerica*, Eddie Redmayne in *The Danish Girl*, Hilary Swank in *Boys Don't Cry*, and Jared Leto in *Dallas Buyers Club*), but rare to cast transgender actors in transgender roles. When Lelio cast Vega as the lead in his movie, they helped change that. Vega's mezzo-soprano singing voice enabled her to sing her own songs in the movie. For her searing performance, she won Chile's prestigious honor, the Caleuche Acting Award for Best Actress, and the Best Actress Award at the Palm Springs International Film Festival, for her portrayal of Marina Vidal, a transgender woman in mourning after the untimely death of her boyfriend. In 2018, Daniela Vega made history by becoming the first openly transgender woman to present at the Oscars, and *A Fantastic Woman* also made history when it became the first Oscar winner to feature a transgender storyline with an openly trans person playing the lead role. *A Fantastic Woman* was also the first Chilean movie to win an Academy Award for Best Foreign Film, making Vega's home country proud.

Time magazine named Vega one of the World's 100 Most Influential People, and Michelle Bachelet, the former President of Chile, praised Vega and the rest of the team who worked on the film. Bachelet posted on Twitter:

"My biggest compliments to @slelio, @ danivega @tengochicle and the whole team #UnaMujerFantástica! The prize, which fills us with pride, not only recognizes a film of great quality, but a history of respect for the diversity that makes us good as a country. #Oscars."

Ellen DeGeneres

Emmy Award-Winning Talk Show Host

"I always say there is a lot more good in the world than there is bad."

F ew public figures have paid a higher price for coming out than Ellen DeGeneres. She graced the cover of *Time* magazine in 1997 with the headline, "Yep, I'm Gay," and her character on the hit TV show, *Ellen*, came out in tandem a couple of weeks later. Her brave proclamation was made during the era of "Don't Ask, Don't Tell" and before same-sex marriage was legal in the States. At the time, the country wasn't ready for an openly lesbian actress playing an openly lesbian lead character on television, and her public revelation resulted in bomb threats, pulled advertising, and ultimately the cancellation of her sitcom a year later. But DeGeneres was never one to give up. Armed with perseverance and a positive attitude, she came back stronger than ever and went on to become one of the most powerful celebrities in the world.

In 2013, DeGeneres won over a slew of new fans when she became the voice of the character Dory in Pixar's hit animated movie, *Finding Nemo*. In that year, she also quickly climbed back up the ratings with a new talk show, *The Ellen DeGeneres Show*. By 2017, she had won thirty Emmys and broken the record for number of People's Choice Awards won, with a total of twenty awards. A Pew Research Center survey found DeGeneres to be the most influential LGBTQ public figure in America, and *Forbes* even added her to "The World's 100 Most Powerful Women" list. DeGeneres is also one of the most influential people on social media. When she hosted the Oscars in 2016, she posted a celebrity-filled selfie pic from the event which was quickly retweeted more than three million times, breaking the record for the most retweeted image and earning three million dollars for charity. DeGeneres is an iconic star known around the world, not only for her self-deprecating humor, but also for her generous heart. She has raised millions of dollars for cancer research, Hurricane Katrina survivors, animal rights and welfare, and various other charities.

She uses her platform to promote the causes she believes in, including animal welfare, healthy eating, anti-bullying, human rights, and LGBTQ equality. She urges her viewers to be kind, acknowledging that her experience of discrimination made her especially aware of the importance of compassion. In 2016, DeGeneres received the highest civilian honor, the Presidential Medal of Freedom. President Barack Obama explained to the audience, "Again and again, Ellen DeGeneres has shown us that a single individual can make the world a more fun, more open, more loving place—so long as we just keep swimming." Obama's words couldn't have been more accurate. Ellen DeGeneres practices what she preaches, and her reach extends far beyond the 3.9 million regular viewers who tune in to her show every weekday. She is now known around the world as much for her kindness as for her humor.

Robin Roberts

Award-Winning News Anchor

"Optimism is a muscle—it gets stronger with use."

Robin Roberts graduated with a Bachelor of Arts degree in Communications from Southern Louisiana University. Combining her education and love of sports, she became a sports reporter for a local television station in Mississippi. As she advanced in her career and became a news anchor, her compassion, transparency, and ability to connect with viewers led her to being voted the "Most Trusted Person on Television" by a 2013 *Reader's Digest* poll. In 1995, Roberts began contributing to *Good Morning America*, and ten years later, ABC hired her as a full-time co-anchor on the show. As a co-anchor, she helped the broadcast become the number-one morning show on television, winning five Emmy Awards and a People's Choice Award. Roberts was also honored with the Walter Cronkite Award for Excellence in Journalism and the George Foster Peabody Award. She was even inducted into the Broadcasting & Cable Hall of Fame. In 2018, she received the Lifetime Achievement Award from the Radio Television Digital News Foundation.

One of the things that sets Roberts apart from so many others in the industry is her ability to wear her heart on her sleeve and emotionally empathize with her viewers. When Hurricane Katrina hit the Gulf Coast of the United States, she was temporarily unable to contact family members, leaving her to wonder if they had survived. Thankfully, they had, but much of her hometown of Pass Christian, Mississippi, was destroyed, including her high school. Because she was personally impacted, when Roberts reported on the storm, viewers affected by the disaster were able to relate to her in a unique way.

In 2012, Roberts experienced a life-changing moment. On the day she was granted an interview with President Barack

Obama about same-sex marriage, Roberts found out she had myelodysplastic syndrome (MDS), a rare disease that attacks a person's blood and bone marrow. Her condition was life-threatening and would require a bone marrow transplant. Stunned by the news, she decided to go ahead with the groundbreaking interview, in which the president reversed his earlier position and endorsed same-sex marriage. That interview probably did more to change hearts and minds than any other. Soon afterward, Roberts decided to go public with the news of her disease and announced on *GMA* that she would be taking a leave of absence to undergo chemotherapy, blood tests, and isolation in preparation for and recovery from a bone marrow transplant. Once again, the viewers connected with Roberts. Her announcement on the show resulted in an 1,800-percent spike in donor registration with the National Marrow Donor Program Match Registry. While going through treatment, she allowed her network to document her journey and build a public service campaign in an effort to raise awareness of the rare disease. Thankfully, Roberts made a full recovery, and came back stronger than ever. It's no wonder she was voted the "Most Trusted Person on Television." She bares her soul and reveals the most intimate moments of her life in order to help other people.

Chris Nee

Emmy Award–Winning Writer and Producer

"It's so powerful to show representation of somebody who's not usually on TV."

C hris Nee began her career as an associate producer at Sesame Street International, and went on to create groundbreaking television show characters for Disney. Some of her earlier writing credits include *Blue's Clues, American Dragon: Jake Long, Johnny and the Sprites, Higglytown Heroes, The Backyardigans, Wonder Pets!,* and *Henry Hugglemonster.* Nee wound up spending a lot of time in the doctor's office while her two-year-old son was being treated for asthma, and it was then that she realized nobody had done a show to help make doctor visits less scary for kids. She came up with an idea for an animated series in which a little girl was a doctor for stuffed animals and broken toys. That show became Disney Junior's *Doc McStuffins,* and with a young, African-American girl interested in science as the main character, it inspired children around the world. The show became an instant hit, as the series premiere attracted 1.08 million viewers ages two to five, prompting *AdWeek* to call the show a "ratings juggernaut." That interest spilled into the toy industry as well. In 2013, *Doc McStuffins* merchandise generated about five hundred million dollars in sales, and according to the *New York Times,* industry experts said that the toys seemed to be "setting a record as the best-selling toy line based on an African-American character."

The show was such a cultural phenomenon that even First Lady Michelle Obama guest-starred in one of the episodes. Following up on the success of *Doc McStuffins,* Nee became Executive Producer on another Disney Junior show called *Vampirina,* based on the *Vampirina Ballerina* book series by Anne Marie Pace. The show is about a young vampire who has to learn how to fit in and make new friends in the human world after moving with her family from Transylvania to Pennsylvania. The show was another instant hit. With an Emmy Award, a Peabody Award, and a Humanitas Prize under her belt, Chris Nee is a powerhouse in the children's television industry, creating shows that inspire young kids and allow them to see themselves represented in the shows they watch.

Sir Ian McKellen

Golden Globe-Winning Actor

"I've never met a gay person who regretted coming out—including myself. Life at last begins to make sense, when you are open and honest."

In Hollywood, many LGBTQ actors stay in the closet because they fear they'll lose fans and/or acting jobs, but Sir Ian McKellen is an example of how one doesn't need to hide who they are in order to have a successful career as an actor. He made his professional debut on stage in *A Man for All Seasons* at the Belgrade Theater in 1961, and went on to star in some of the biggest blockbuster movie franchises in the world. McKellen has played numerous roles over the last few decades, but his most notable film roles include James Whale in *Gods and Monsters*, Magneto in the *X-Men* films, Gandalf in *The Lord of the Rings* and *The Hobbit* trilogies, Sir Leigh Teabing in *The Da Vinci Code*, Sherlock Holmes in *Mr. Holmes*, and Cogsworth in Disney's live-action version of *Beauty and the Beast*. He has won numerous awards including a Critics' Choice Movie Award, a Golden Globe Award, a Saturn Award, a Screen Actors Guild Award, and a Tony Award. During a 1988 interview with BBC Radio 3, McKellen publicly came out as a gay man while speaking out against Section 28, a bill that banned the promotion of homosexuality in the UK and made it illegal to discuss homosexuality in schools in a positive way. He continued speaking out for equality, and later that year, with other activists, he helped found Stonewall, an LGBTQ charity in the UK, named after the riots in New York.

In addition to helping the LGBTQ community, McKellen has also done charity work to raise money for earthquake victims, to support the arts, to end homelessness, to help the elderly, to raise awareness for prostate cancer, and much more. He was even knighted by Queen Elizabeth II for his service to the performing arts. It's safe to say that McKellen is more than just an actor. He's a successful actor who has helped make the world a better place.

Margaret Cho

Actress and Award-Winning Comedian

*"The power of visibility can never
be underestimated."*

B orn and raised in San Francisco, Margaret Cho, who is openly bisexual, grew up around an eclectic group of people from all walks of life, and because of this, she is able to connect with those who feel marginalized in society. She uses this to her benefit in her stand-up routines, speaking out against racism, sexism, and homophobia. Cho has fought long and hard to be legitimately recognized in an industry dominated by straight white men. Over the course of her career, people criticized her looks and characteristics, calling her too fat and too Asian, but she never let that stop her. When people tried to knock her down, she came back stronger and better than ever, like a phoenix rising from the ashes.

When she was sixteen years old, Cho started her career at a comedy club above a bookstore run by her parents. The unfiltered comedian got her big break in 1991, when she won a comedy competition, the first prize being an opportunity to open for Jerry Seinfeld. Her fan base continued to grow, and in 1994, she won the American Comedy Award for Funniest Female Stand-Up Comic. Cho's success led to her starring in her own TV show, *All-American Girl*, a sitcom in which she played a rebellious teenager in a traditional Korean-American family. The show took a toll on her, though, with producers telling her she was "too Asian" at times and "not Asian enough" at others. They even had the gall to hire a coach so she could learn how to be "more Asian." Cho was also criticized by producers about her weight, leading her to go on a crash diet and lose thirty pounds in just two weeks. The rapid weight loss was unhealthy and resulted in years of serious kidney problems.

Cho turned to drugs and alcohol when the show was canceled. After sobering up, she wrote about the struggles she had faced while filming *All-American Girl*, and turned it into an autobiography and a one-woman comedy show called *I'm the One That I Want*. Her material dealt with issues like race, weight, body image, eating disorders, and substance abuse. The show was a hit, and was released as a concert film the following year.

Cho would later go on to appear in numerous comedy specials, movies, and television shows, including a guest appearance on *30 Rock*, where her performance earned her an Emmy nomination. In 2017, *Rolling Stone* named her one of the "50 Best Stand-Up Comics of All Time."

When she's not making people laugh, Cho fights racism, sexism, homophobia, homelessness, and more. She has performed at rallies for equal rights, and even done pop-up charity performances on street corners to help the homeless. On April 30, 2008, San Francisco Mayor Gavin Newsom officially declared it Margaret Cho Day.

Margaret Cho is fighting the good fight, and has inspired marginalized communities along the way. Through her activism and comedy, she has proven that you can't keep a good girl down.

The Wachowskis

Award-Winning Directors, Producers, and Writers

Lilly

Lana

"The way a film can change over the generations… The movie changes, because we change as individuals."

–Lilly Wachowski

"I couldn't find anyone like me in the world and it felt like my dreams were foreclosed simply because my gender was less typical than others."

–Lana Wachowski

L ana and Lilly Wachowski are Hollywood juggernauts. They made their directorial debut in 1996 with *Bound*, a movie that is believed to be the first mainstream Hollywood film to put a lesbian relationship front and center without making it the main point of the story. After their success with *Bound*, they went on to create one of the most critically acclaimed sci-fi movies ever made. The Wachowskis wrote and directed the blockbuster phenomenon, *The Matrix*. The movie is probably best known for popularizing a visual effect known as "bullet time," in which high-speed actions (such as flying bullets) occur in slow motion while the camera's viewpoint moves through the scene at normal speed. *The Matrix* won numerous awards including four Academy Awards, two BAFTA Awards, three MTV Movie Awards, and two Saturn Awards. The movie was so successful, it spawned two sequels, and even expanded into comic books, video games, and animated short films. Because of the its significant cultural, artistic, and historic achievements, *The Matrix* was selected for preservation in the National Film Registry of the Library of Congress. After completing the *Matrix* trilogy, the Wachowskis went on to produce and write the film adaptation of Alan Moore's graphic novel *V for Vendetta*. They also wrote, directed, and produced *Speed Racer*, *Cloud Atlas*, and *Jupiter Ascending* before writing and directing the Emmy-nominated Netflix series, *Sense8*.

Lana made global headlines when she became the first major Hollywood director to publicly come out as transgender. Her sister, Lilly, also publicly came out as a transgender woman a few years later. The siblings, who have worked side by side throughout their careers, have also been each other's support system along the way, and by living their lives authentically, they became role models for many people around the world.

Part 5

GOVERNMENT & MILITARY

Jóhanna Sigurðardóttir

Iceland's First Female Prime Minister and the World's First Openly LGBTQ Head of Government

"A society that does not use the intellectual power of its female population fully is not a wise society."

Jóhanna Sigurðardóttir was born in 1942 in Reykjavik, Iceland's capital and largest city. She was elected to Iceland's parliament in 1978 and became the Minister of Social Affairs and Social Security in 1987.

After losing an internal election for the leadership of the Social Democratic Party in 1994, she went on to form her own party, National Awakening. It eventually merged with the Social Democratic Party, the People's Alliance, and the Women's List to form the Social Democratic Alliance.

On February 1, 2009, Jóhanna Sigurðardóttir made history by becoming Iceland's first female prime minister and the world's first openly LGBTQ head of government. She was also the country's longest-serving Member of Parliament during her time in office.

When Sigurðardóttir took over as PM, Iceland had just experienced the worst financial disaster in its history. She is widely credited with restoring the economy and bringing back prosperity to the island nation by bolstering tourism and implementing stronger oversight measures in the banking industry. She exemplified Iceland's values of openness, fairness, and social responsibility.

When Iceland legalized marriage equality in 2010, Sigurðardóttir married author and playwright, Jónína Leósdóttir, making them one of the first same-sex couples to marry in the country. They had been in a civil union since 2002.

Sigurðardóttir helped bring Iceland out of a grave financial crisis, crediting her success to getting more women in government roles, thus making the administration more gender-balanced and creating a working government with a shared power structure. It's no wonder that, in the year Sigurðardóttir became prime minister, Iceland ranked number one on the World Economic Forum's annual Global Gender Gap Index, a report that measures equity in education, employment, politics, and health. Forbes also listed Sigurðardóttir as one of the 100 Most Powerful Women in the world that year, coming in at number seventy-five.

Leo Varadkar

First Openly Gay Prime Minister of Ireland

*"Politicians should trust people with the truth.
Very often, we don't do that."*

B orn in Ireland in 1979, Leo Varadkar is the son of an Indian doctor and an Irish nurse. In 2017, when he was only thirty-eight years old, he was elected Taoiseach (Irish prime minister), becoming the youngest person to hold that position. He also became the first Irish government leader of an ethnic minority background, the first openly gay Irish government minister, and the world's fourth openly gay head of government in modern times, joining Luxembourg Prime Minister Xavier, former Belgian Prime Minister Elio Di Rupo, and former Icelandic Prime Minister Jóhanna Sigurðardóttir.

Before rising to Taoiseach, Varadkar was Minister of Transport, Tourism, and Sport, and led one of the most successful tourism initiatives in Irish History. "The Gathering," was a staging of five thousand events aimed at attracting members of the Irish diaspora, including the thirty-five million in the US alone, and other visitors to Ireland, a country of five million. During Varadkar's tenure, the number of international visitors to Ireland increased by one million per year.

Varadkar publicly came out as a gay man a few months before Ireland voted on a referendum to define marriage as a legal union between two people regardless of sex, and he became a champion for the cause. During this time, he held the position of Minister for Health, and his high-profile role helped put a human face to the matter. He went on to eloquently defend marriage equality in the Dáil Éireann (Ireland's equivalent of Parliament or Congress), saying, "We believe in marriage as an institution, and so we believe equal marriage makes it stronger and makes society stronger too." When Election Day arrived, 62 percent of voters cast their ballots in favor of marriage equality, and Ireland became the first country in the world to approve same-sex marriage by popular vote.

One of Varadkar's first acts as Taoiseach was to announce a referendum to repeal Ireland's Eighth Amendment, a law that gave "the unborn" the same rights as mothers, and thus effectively banned almost all abortions. Varadkar put his support behind the repeal, and on May 25, 2018, with voter turnout at a near-historic high, the Irish people voted 66.4 percent in favor of removing the ban from the Constitution.

Even though Ireland has long been considered one of Europe's most socially conservative countries, Varadkar has helped liberalize policy on some of their key social issues. He represents a new wave of Irish politics, attempting to ensure economic prosperity, social equality, and health, while holding firm to the "law and order" tenets of the Fine Gail party.

Eric Fanning

Former Secretary of the United States Army

"America's diversity is our army's strength."

E ric Fanning became the first openly gay Secretary of the Army (and the highest-ranking openly LGBTQ official ever employed at the Pentagon) when President Obama appointed him on May 18, 2016. In this role, he was responsible for all matters relating to the United States Army, including recruiting, training, personnel, reserve affairs, installations, environmental issues, weapons systems, equipment acquisition, communications, and financial management.

Fanning came from a military family, and growing up, he thought about following in their footsteps and signing up for the armed forces too, but gay people were not allowed to serve in the military and he didn't want to serve in silence. Instead, he took on civilian roles and never actually *served* in the military himself. So how did he become the Secretary of the Army if he never actually served? For separation-of-powers reasons, the United States has civilian control of the military.

The Army is not the only branch of the military that Fanning worked with. In total, Fanning held high-level civilian jobs in three branches of the military, and prior to becoming the Secretary of the Army, he also held positions as Deputy Under Secretary of the Navy, Acting Secretary of the Air Force, and Chief of Staff to the Secretary of Defense.

Fanning felt that being gay gave him a perspective that helped bring a focus to inclusivity and diversity in the army. He believed diversity was an asset, and that the army would be stronger if it looked like society. Because of this, he implemented policies to help the army reflect that belief. During his tenure, he issued grooming and dress waivers to

Sikhs and Muslims for religious reasons, and even helped the Pentagon end its formal ban on women in combat roles.

Eric Fanning helped break a glass ceiling for the LGBTQ community and the United States military is stronger because of his involvement.

Technical Sergeant Leonard P. Matlovich

Vietnam War Veteran and Recipient of the Purple Heart and the Bronze Star

"When I was in the military they gave me a medal for killing two men, and a discharge for loving one."

Leonard P. Matlovich was born in Savannah, Georgia, on July 6, 1943. At age nineteen, he followed in his father's footsteps and enlisted in the United States Air Force, where he served for twelve years. During his tenure, he taught race relations classes to combat racism in the Air Force, served three tours of duty in Vietnam, and was awarded both the Bronze Star and the Purple Heart.

In 1975, he purposely outed himself to the Air Force to create a test case for challenging the ban on gays and lesbians serving in the military. Despite being a well-loved and well-decorated officer who served his country for over a decade, he was discharged in 1975 because of his sexual orientation. Matlovich fought this in court for years, and became a national hero along the way, appearing on the cover of *Time* magazine and the front page of the *New York Times*. He also appeared on numerous talk shows and news programs before eventually settling with the Air Force out of court.

Because his fight against discrimination in the military made him a household name, equal rights groups asked Matlovich to help with other LGBTQ causes. When Anita Bryant ran a Florida campaign to repeal a local ordinance prohibiting discrimination on the basis of sexual orientation, Matlovich helped campaigns fight against her. He also stepped up to battle the Briggs initiative, which tried to ban gay and lesbian people from teaching in California public schools. And when California tried to pass Proposition 64 (a bill that would have required people with HIV/AIDS to be isolated and quarantined), Matlovich protested against that, too.

Because of his dedicated service in the military, his fight for LGBTQ equality, and his mission to help people living with HIV and AIDS, Leonard P. Matlovich is still a hero to many people today. His tombstone, which is located in the Congressional Cemetery in Washington, does not have his name inscribed on it because he wanted it to be a memorial for all gay veterans. Instead, it bears the quote, "When I was in the military they gave me a medal for killing two men, and a discharge for loving one." Many LGBTQ veterans have chosen to be buried near him, and his gravesite became a symbol of hope during the fight to repeal Don't Ask, Don't Tell. It continues to be a symbol of hope today.

Part 6

MUSIC

Sir Elton John

Grammy Award-Winning Singer, Songwriter, and Composer

"Better to build a bridge than a wall."

When it comes to music, Sir Elton John (born Reginald Kenneth Dwight on March 25, 1947) is one of the most iconic people in the industry. He's a singer, songwriter, and composer who taught himself how to play the piano when he was only four years old.

John took the music industry by storm, and with the help of various lyricists, such as Bernie Taupin, Tim Rice, and Gary Osborne, he spewed out a string of hits, making him one of the most popular musicians of the twentieth century. He dominated the singles charts, and even branched out into movie soundtracks and musicals. His song "Can You Feel the Love Tonight" (written for Disney's animated movie, *The Lion King*) won Best Original Song for both the Academy Awards and the Golden Globe Awards. He later teamed up with Lee Hall to adapt the movie *Billy Elliott* into a musical, and that show went on to win ten Tony Awards.

In 1997, John released a rewritten version of his song "Candle in the Wind" as a tribute to his friend Diana, Princess of Wales, who had died in a horrific car accident. The single sold thirty-three million copies worldwide, and the proceeds went to Diana's charities. The Guinness World Records website lists it as the best-selling single since the US and UK singles charts began in the 1950s.

In addition to his musical success, John also contributes to various causes. Most notably, he created the Elton John AIDS Foundation to help raise money for education programs, direct care, and support services to those living with, or at high risk of contracting, HIV.

Other highlights of Elton John's career include receiving the Grammy Legend Award, induction into the Rock and Roll Hall of Fame, and ranking as the most successful male solo artist on the Billboard Hot 100 "Top 10 Artists of All Time" list in 2013. With all his success and contributions to the world, it's no wonder Queen Elizabeth dubbed him a knight.

John married his longtime partner, David Furnish, when same-sex marriage became legal in the UK. They have two children together.

k.d. lang

Grammy Award-Winning Singer and Songwriter

"Look. Art knows no prejudice, art knows no boundaries, art doesn't really have judgment in its purest form. So just go, just go."

Nashville loved k.d. lang's voice, but didn't really know what to make of her. Born in 1961 in Alberta, Canada, she marched to her own drum and did things the way she wanted to. Some of her choices paid off, while some angered fans and caused boycotts. Still, lang rose to fame with her talent while never compromising her values.

In 1985, she won her first JUNO Award for Most Promising Female Vocalist, leading her to sign with an American record producer in Nashville, Tennessee, and release the critically acclaimed album, *Angel with a Lariat*. 1988 seemed to be her year, winning a Grammy Award for Best Country Collaboration with Vocals for "Crying" (a duet she did with Roy Orbison), being selected as the "Woman of the Year" by Canadian women's magazine *Chatelaine*, and garnering international recognition for her performance at the closing ceremony of the Calgary Winter Olympics.

With her androgynous style, lang continued her rise to fame, winning the Entertainer of the Year award from the Canadian Country Music Association three years in a row (1987-1989) and Female Artist of the Year in 1988 and 1989. There seemed to be no stopping her… until she joined a "Meat Stinks" campaign for PETA. "We all love animals," lang said in the ad, "but why do we call some of them pets and some of them dinner? If you knew how meat was made, you'd probably lose your lunch. I know, I'm from cattle country. That's why I became a vegetarian."

The backlash from "cattle country" was immediate and harsh. A sign identifying Consort, Alberta as the "Home of k.d. lang" was burned down, and various radio stations in Canada and the United States started pulling her music from the air. The boycott didn't hinder lang for long. In 1992, she came out as a lesbian in the June edition of the *Advocate*, and crossed music genres with the release of her album Ingénue. Her single "Constant Craving" became the biggest hit of her career, earning her another Grammy for Best Female Pop Vocal Performance.

Even though lang had experienced backlash for being an animal rights activist, that didn't stop her from continuing to speak out on issues she felt were important. She has since become an activist for LGBTQ equality, HIV/AIDS, and Tibetan human rights.

Her career continued to thrive, landing on VH-1's list of the 100 Greatest Women in Rock & Roll and CMT's list of the 40 Greatest Women in Country Music. She has a star on Canada's Walk of Fame, and in 2013, she was inducted into the Canadian Music Hall of Fame. Known for being true to herself and always standing up for what she believes in, k.d. lang has become a legend.

Leonard Bernstein

Tony and Grammy Award–Winning Composer

"This will be our reply to violence: to make music more intensely, more beautifully, more devotedly than ever before."

Probably the greatest American composer, Leonard Bernstein defied classical music convention. He was classically trained at Harvard University and the Curtis Institute of Music, yet he wrote compositions for Broadway. He popularized Mahler's symphonies in the US, yet he peppered his pioneering television series, *Young People's Concerts with the New York Philharmonic,* with music from the Kinks.

Bernstein will probably be best remembered for his musical composition of the Tony Award-winning show *West Side Story,* a musical whose film adaptation won numerous Academy Awards. The modern beats he crafted, combined with bold and provocative social commentary, signaled a new beginning in musical theater. But Bernstein was so much more than a Broadway musical composer, having composed a violin concerto, three symphonies, and two operas. He also collaborated with Jerome Robbins to compose ballets and wrote the score for the award-winning film *On the Waterfront.*

As Bernstein was becoming better known around the world, rumors about his sexuality began to spread. Fearing that his career would suffer as a result, his mentor Mitropoulos suggested he get married. Even though Bernstein did get married and had three children with Chilean actress, Felicia Montealegre, it was no secret that he loved men. His wife even wrote in a letter, "You are a homosexual...our marriage is not based on passion but on tenderness and mutual respect."

Bernstein had a long-lasting friendship with the Kennedys. He was invited to participate in JFK's preinaugural gala, and conducted the National Symphony Orchestra in a piece he composed specifically for the event. He even participated in fundraisers with the Kennedys, including one event that helped raise money for the building now known as the John F. Kennedy Center for the Performing Arts. After JFK's assassination, Bernstein conducted Mahler's Symphony No. 2, Resurrection, in a televised memorial for the president. He performed again at Robert Kennedy's funeral in 1968.

During his career, Bernstein won sixteen Grammy Awards and multiple Tony Awards, and became a member of the American Theater Hall of Fame, but in addition to his musical contributions, Bernstein was also dedicated to making the world a better place. He won many prizes throughout his life and donated much of any prize money to humanitarian causes ranging from AIDS awareness and research to world peace. In 1989, he famously conducted the Berlin Celebration Concerts on both sides of the Berlin Wall as it was being dismantled.

Bernstein's impact was recognized around the world, and he has numerous decorations from the governments of Austria, Chile, Finland, France, West Germany, Italy, Israel, and Mexico. He truly is one of the greats.

Michael Tilson Thomas

World-Renowned Conductor, Composer, and Pianist

"The world changes when there's music in it."

Michael Tilson Thomas was destined for glory. He was born in 1944, the grandson of the great Yiddish theater actors, the Tomashevskys, and the son of a Hollywood producer. He began learning piano at age three. By age twenty-four, he became the youngest assistant conductor in the history of the Boston Symphony Orchestra, and by 2013, he was an eleven-time Grammy Award Winner.

Tilson Thomas became Music Director of the San Francisco Symphony in 1995. Known for its diverse repertory and range of classical music, he elevated the San Francisco Symphony to national prominence, joining the company of the great symphony orchestras of New York, Chicago, Boston, and Los Angeles. As a guest conductor of the London Symphony and a regular maestro with some of the world's great orchestras, he is renowned for his technical precision and unbridled passion for the composers whose music he embraces. Nearly singlehandedly, Tilson Thomas has brought American composers into prominence, highlighting the works of John Adams, Leonard Bernstein, John Cage, Aaron Copland, George Gershwin, Charles Ives, and Steve Reich.

In addition to conducting, Tilson Thomas is dedicated to educating and inspiring young musicians. In 1987, he founded the New World Symphony, an academy where the most gifted musical graduates are trained for leadership roles in professional orchestras and ensembles. Later, in conjunction with the San Francisco Symphony, he created *Keeping Score*, a television and radio series designed to make classical music accessible to all. It later incorporated an online component providing K–12 teachers a model for classroom arts integration.

In 2009, Tilson Thomas partnered with YouTube to create
the world's first online collaborative orchestra. Musicians
from all over the world uploaded their audition videos for a
chance to play at Carnegie Hall under the direction of Tilson
Thomas. Finalists were voted on by the YouTube community,
and, by the time of the official concert date, the audition tapes
had been viewed over fifteen million times. The event was so
popular, auditions for the YouTube Symphony Orchestra were
held again in 2011, with the winners playing together at the
Sydney Opera House.

Tilson Thomas has left an indelible imprint on the world
of classical music, and has been widely recognized for his
significant contributions to the arts. In addition to his eleven
Grammys and numerous other awards, he is also a Chevalier
dans l'Ordre des Arts et des Lettres of France, and a recipient
of the National Medal of Arts. Tilson Thomas is the most
prominent openly gay conductor of our time, and arguably one
of the greatest conductors in modern history.

Ricky Martin

Actor and Grammy Award-Winning Singer

"If we, who are all here together on this earth, don't take care of one another, then who else will? It is our duty."

From his early days singing in the teen group Menudo to becoming a Grammy Award-winning international pop star, Ricky Martin is hands-down one of the biggest Latin music stars in the world. He's known for his good looks, charming personality, generous heart, sexy dance moves, and of course, a distinctive, energetic voice that got the whole world to shake their *bon-bons*.

Born Enrique Jose Martin Morales IV, Ricky Martin sang for five years with the teen group Menudo before aging out at eighteen. He then focused on his solo acting and singing career. He had a recurring role on ABC's daytime soap opera, *General Hospital*, and he starred in the Broadway stage production of Les Misérables.

Martin was already well-known throughout the Latin and Hispanic communities from his early Menudo days and a few solo music albums in Spanish, but when he performed "La Copa de la Vida" ("The Cup of Life") at the 1998 World Cup soccer tournament in France, he suddenly became an international sensation. That performance was broadcast to two billion people around the world and became an instant hit. He performed the song again at the 1999 Grammy Awards, where he picked up an award for Best Latin Pop Performance. Martin continued to release hits, including the English single, "Livin' La Vida Loca," and his debut English album *Ricky Martin* (which debuted at number one on the Billboard chart), and because of his long-lasting success, Martin received a star on the Hollywood Walk of Fame on October 16, 2007.

In his spare time, Martin uses his fame to help those in need. He became a UNICEF Goodwill Ambassador and has worked to improve the rights of children worldwide. He also founded the Ricky Martin Foundation, which helps defend youth and fight against child exploitation and human trafficking. His philanthropic efforts don't stop there, though. He also helped with 2005 tsunami relief efforts in Thailand and with the 2017 hurricane relief efforts in Puerto Rico.

Martin also has a long history of helping in the fight against HIV/AIDS. He was a spokesperson for MAC's Viva Glam campaign (supporting organizations that provide services to people living with HIV/AIDS) and in 2016, he even auctioned off a passionate kiss at an amfAR charity event in Brazil. Guess how much that kiss went for: a whopping ninety thousand dollars!

In 2010, Ricky Martin came out of the closet by publishing an announcement on his website. "I am proud to say that I am a fortunate homosexual man. I am very blessed to be who I am." He now lives with his husband and two children.

Rob Halford

Lead Vocalist for the Grammy Award-Winning Heavy Metal Band, Judas Priest

"I think the last thing you want in life is to live with regret."

In 1998, Rob Halford shocked the world by coming out as a gay man during an interview with MTV. Sure, there had been other people in the music industry who were open about their sexuality at the time, but Halford was a heavy metal singer, and the genre was known for its aggression and hypermasculinity. Many people believed that a person could not be both gay and masculine, but Halford helped chip away at that stereotype.

Halford was born on August 25, 1951, in Sutton Coldfield, a town in England. In the early 1970s, he joined Judas Priest as lead singer, and the band went on to become one of the most influential metal bands in the world. The use of twin guitar harmonies, fast double bass drums, and high-pitched vocals distinguished the band from its contemporaries, and the versatility of Halford's voice, going from a deep throaty growl to an operatic, screaming falsetto, made their music instantly recognizable.

In addition to their music, Judas Priest also became trendsetters in fashion. They had an extreme biker look onstage as early as 1978, wearing leather and studs from head to toe. Their look influenced the style of other bands such as Metallica, Slipknot, and more.

Halford left Judas Priest in 1992 to pursue other projects. During his time away, he was the lead singer of Fight, 2wo (sometimes referred to as Two), and Halford before returning as lead singer of Judas Priest in 2003. His coming out as a gay man did not hinder the band in any way; in fact, they went on to win a Grammy in 2009 for Best Metal Performance with their album *Dissident Aggressor*.

As frontman for Judas Priest and one of the first openly gay metal stars, Rob Halford is a true pioneer in the music industry.

Part 7

RELIGION

Archbishop Carl Bean

Religious Leader

Carl Bean on the left.

"My life is testimony to one statement and one statement only: God is love, and love is for everybody."

Archbishop Carl Bean was born into a life of poverty but after years of adversity, he would go on to become a leader in the community, spreading hope and light to those around him. He released the surprise Motown hit, "I Was Born This Way," in the 1970s, and the unique song featured Bean belting out his pride in being gay. That was something the music industry hadn't really heard before, and the gay disco anthem spread through the clubs like wildfire. The song catapulted him to fame and led him to work with musical legends such as Dionne Warwick, Burt Bacharach, Miles Davis, and Sammy Davis Jr. But it was during the early 1980s that Bean found his true calling: serving others as an openly gay ordained minister during the height of the AIDS crisis.

Bean founded the Unity Fellowship of Christ Church, a church for openly gay and lesbian African-Americans. He also created the Minority AIDS Project through the church, the first community-based HIV/AIDS organization established and managed by people of color in the United States. The Project provided housing, transportation, outreach, HIV prevention, HIV testing, case management, and mental health services.

"In the gay community, they said Silence = Death," Bean told *POZ* magazine. "That personally spoke to me, that you can't be silent now, you can't let people die around you. I just knew I had love for my fellow human beings and that the Christ consciousness in me said, 'I am my brother's keeper.'"

The church continues to spread Bean's message that "God Is Love and Love Is For Everyone." As for his music, "I Was Born This Way" made a comeback after being remixed in the 1980s, and the song has been remixed multiple times since then. Bean's message of love and self-acceptance continues to resonate with people across the country.

Bishop Gene Robinson

First Openly Gay Bishop Elected to the Episcopal Church

"It seems to me that if God calls us to anything it's to a life of integrity."

Twelve years before the Supreme Court legalized same-sex marriage in the United States, something significant happened. At the time, there were no federal hate crime protections for LGBTQ people, and "Don't Ask, Don't Tell" was in full effect, banning gays and lesbians from openly serving in the military. Thirteen states still had sodomy laws in place, giving them a legal way to persecute people in the community. Even with all the animosity against those who identified as LGBTQ, Gene Robinson was elected bishop by the New Hampshire diocese in 2003, paving the way for him to become the first openly gay person to be a consecrated bishop in the Episcopal Church.

His elevation to bishop upset many and created a schism in the church, resulting in approximately one hundred thousand people leaving for the more conservative Anglican Church in North America. Regardless, Robinson risked everything, including his safety, for what he believed he was called to do. In November of 2003, he was officially consecrated in front of an audience of four thousand, including his parents, former wife, children, and partner. During the ceremony, Robinson was surrounded by bodyguards, and even had to wear a bulletproof vest under his robes because of the death threats he was getting. Those death threats continued for years and ultimately played a big role in his decision to retire in 2013. Before retiring, though, he led a very public life doing good in the name of the church.

During his time as a church leader, Robinson was an AIDS educator in both the US and Africa. He also spent a lot of time ministering to those in prison and was an advocate for many causes, including racial equality, debt relief for impoverished nations, socially responsible investment, and access to health care for the uninsured. In addition, Robinson lobbied for full civil marriage rights and equal protection under the law for all LGBTQ people. He even advised Barack Obama on LGBTQ equality issues during his first presidential campaign and delivered the invocation at President Obama's inauguration.

Robinson has inspired people around the world to hope. His story was featured in the documentary *For the Bible Tells Me So*, which won numerous awards, including Best Documentary at the Seattle International Film Festival and the Grand Jury Prize at the 2007 Sundance Film Festival. He has done much more than lead the Episcopal Church. Robinson has helped many people feel welcomed in a place where they previously felt ostracized. He helped make the Episcopal Church a beacon of inclusion.

Part 8

SCIENCE

Alan Turing

War Hero and Father of Computer Science

"Sometimes it is the people who no one imagines anything of who do the things that no one can imagine."

It was the height of World War II, the deadliest war in history, resulting in more than fifty million deaths. The Germans were using the Enigma machine as their primary way of ciphering messages and war commands. Their superior encryption technology was giving them an upper hand in the war until Alan Turing, a gay man, cracked the code and helped turn the tide of the war.

Turing, born on June 23, 1912 in London, England, was one of the greatest mathematical minds of the twentieth century. He attended the University of Cambridge and received a PhD from Princeton University. He then took a job at the Government Code and Cypher School (GCCS), where he led a team of code breakers instrumental in ending WWII.

During the war, German U-boats were intercepting cargoes of essential supplies for Great Britain. Turing broke the Enigma code they were using to exchange critical information, enabling Britain to determine the location of the U-boats and thus avoid or destroy them. Turing and his team helped decode numerous other intercepted messages, too, giving the Allies the upper hand in the war. Some military historians believe that Turing helped shorten the war by two or more years, and that, without his efforts, an estimated two million more lives would have been lost. Because of his significant code-breaking work, he was made an Officer of the Most Excellent Order of the British Empire.

All of this is impressive on its own, but Alan Turing was more than just a code-breaker. He also came up with a hypothetical machine capable of computing anything that is computable, basically an early concept of a programmable digital computer.

So basically, if you've ever typed on a computer or smartphone, you can thank Turing for making that possible.

Sadly, though, Turing was a victim of his time. In 1952, he called the police to report a break-in, but when they found out he had a sexual relationship with the perpetrator, Turing was charged with "gross indecency" for being gay and was given the choice of either going to prison or undergoing chemical castration. He chose the latter. Because of his conviction, Turing also lost his security clearance and, as a result, was no longer allowed to work at the GCCS. What a great way to treat a war hero, right?

Almost sixty years after his death, Turing was posthumously granted a royal pardon by Queen Elizabeth II. Not long after that, the British government passed Turing's Law, posthumously pardoning gay and bisexual men who had been convicted for homosexual acts in the past. We've come a long way since the British government punished Turing for being gay. If he were alive today, how do you think he would feel knowing that the world's largest technology company, Apple, is run by Tim Cook, an openly gay man?

Dr. Marci Bowers

First Openly Transgender Gender-Reassignment Surgeon in the World

"If we're honest with ourselves and each other, I think it finally gives us the opportunity to finally live freely and peacefully."

D r. Marci Bowers has an impressive resume. She trained as an OB-GYN at University of Washington Medical School, where she was voted Chief Resident, and at the University of Minnesota Medical School, where she served as both class president and student body president. After going through gender confirmation surgery in 1997, she decided to advance her medical training and learn to perform the surgery on others, becoming the first openly transgender surgeon in the world to perform this life-changing procedure.

While Bowers spends most of her professional time helping people in the transgender community, she realized that her expertise could also be used to help women and girls around the world who were forced to go through female genital mutilation (FGM), a procedure that involves cutting the female genitalia for non-medical reasons. According to UNICEF, more than two hundred million girls and women have been subjected to FGM in thirty countries, forty-four million of them under the age of fifteen. The violent practice exists predominantly in certain countries in Africa and the Middle East, and often results in complications such as severe pain, hemorrhaging, infection, psychological problems, increased risk of childbirth complications, and, in extreme cases, death. Even though this practice is traumatizing to the victims, it is often carried out because of religious beliefs, cultural tradition, and as a way to prepare young girls for adulthood.

There are only a handful of physicians worldwide who perform FGM reversal surgeries, and Dr. Bowers is one of them. As part of her humanitarian efforts, she has done them free of charge in San Francisco, and has even traveled to Kenya to perform them. In Nairobi, she trained six local doctors in the pioneering techniques so that they could carry on the important work after she returned to the States.

When not performing surgeries, Dr. Bowers is a frequent speaker at international conferences, TED Talks, and medical schools. She has appeared on *Oprah*, *Megyn Kelly Today*, *The Tyra Banks Show*, and in numerous documentaries. She uses her platform to raise awareness of FGM and to educate people on transgender issues. She is a role model who promotes acceptance and helps people around the world get back their sense of themselves.

Sally Ride, PhD

First American Woman in Space

"You can't be what you can't see."

All of NASA's astronauts used to be men. That was until Dr. Sally Ride and five other women were chosen to join NASA's astronaut class in 1978. Dr. Ride eventually became the first American woman to go into space when she flew on the space shuttle Challenger on June 18, 1983.

It took a while for NASA to adapt to having female astronauts. In addition to suggesting women take one hundred tampons with them for a one-week flight in space, NASA engineers also assumed women would want to bring special makeup kits on the journey, and asked Dr. Ride to help them develop one. The press didn't know what to think about women going into space, either. They wanted to know if the flight would affect Dr. Ride's reproductive organs and whether she cried when they had malfunctions in the simulator. Even though Dr. Ride had a doctorate in physics and was clearly capable of doing the same work as her male co-workers, many people focused on her gender rather than her qualifications.

Despite the misconceptions people had regarding female astronauts, Dr. Ride proved that she was more than capable of doing her job. She served in space on two flights, was appointed to help investigate space shuttle disasters, and even led the task force responsible for NASA's long-range and strategic planning.

Dr. Ride retired from NASA in 1987 and went on to teach at Stanford, and later at the University of California, San Diego. In 2001, she founded Sally Ride Science with her partner, Tam O'Shaughnessy, and a small group of their colleagues. The company was created to motivate girls and young women to pursue careers in science, technology, engineering, and math.

Dr. Ride died of pancreatic cancer in 2012, and just before she passed away, she left the decision to make her sexual orientation public to O'Shaughnessy, her partner of twenty-seven years. Dr. Ride's obituary listed O'Shaughnessy as her surviving partner.

Even after her death, Dr. Ride's legacy continues to inspire people. President Barack Obama posthumously awarded her the Presidential Medal of Freedom (the nation's highest civilian honor), and the US Navy named a research vessel after her. Ray Mabus, Secretary of the Navy, said he named the ship after Dr. Ride to "encourage generations of students to continue exploring, discovering, and reaching for the stars." The US Postal Service also created a stamp with Dr. Ride's image on it, saying that she "inspired the nation as a pioneering astronaut, brilliant physicist, and dedicated educator." Dr. Sally Ride isn't just a role model to the LGBTQ community; she's one of America's greatest heroes.

Part 9

SPORTS

Abby Wambach

International Soccer's All-Time Leading Scorer

"Soccer didn't make me who I was. I brought who I was to soccer. And I get to bring who I am wherever I go. And guess what? So do you."

Abby Wambach was born in 1980 in Rochester, New York, and was the youngest of seven children. She joined her first soccer team at age five and, after scoring twenty-seven goals in only three games, was quickly transferred to a boys' league. Wambach continued to play throughout high school and college, and set school career records for goals, assists, and points while playing for the University of Florida Gators. She was drafted into the Women's United Soccer Association in 2002, and by the end of her professional career she had scored an incredible 184 goals, the most ever for any professional male or female player in the history of international soccer.

Wambach is a legend and a role model of power and strength. Along with her US teammates, she won two Olympic gold medals, one at the 2004 Olympic Games in Athens and one at the 2012 Olympic Games in London. She was also voted 2012 FIFA Player of the year. After her team won the 2015 FIFA Women's World Cup, President Obama honored them at the White House, saying they "taught all of America's children that 'playing like a girl' means you're a badass."

But even with a record number of goals, two Olympic gold medals, a World Cup trophy, and numerous awards, Wambach was still paid significantly less than the male soccer players she outperformed. To put it into perspective, Cristiano Ronaldo's salary was more than forty-eight million dollars (not including endorsements) in 2014, while Wambach's annual salary was around two hundred thousand dollars. That's less than half a percent of what Ronaldo made. The pay gap between men and women in professional soccer is staggering.

Wambach admits to not doing enough during her career to fight pay inequity, but has since made it her mission to raise awareness of the issue and fight to change it. She mentioned equal pay during her acceptance speech for the 2016 ESPYs Icon Award, and gave details about the sport's sexist inequalities during her 2018 Commencement Speech at Barnard College, where she received a standing ovation. At a *Fortune* women's conference, Wambach declared, "Enough is enough." Now her mission is to ensure that "playing like a girl" and "playing like a badass" are equally rewarded.

Billie Jean King

Tennis Champion and Pioneer
for Social Justice

"A champion is afraid of losing. Everyone else is afraid of winning."

Billie Jean King had an epiphany when she was twelve years old, playing on the public tennis courts in Long Beach. Everybody wore white—white clothes, white shoes, white socks—and everyone who played was white as well. Seeing the lack of diversity in the sport, she became determined to fight for equal rights and opportunities for boys and girls. King made it her life commitment to ensure that people could play tennis no matter their country of origin, their gender, or their race. But the disparity in sports was great, and in order to have the ability to make a difference, King felt she had to be the best in her field. As time would tell, that's exactly what she became…the best.

King is now considered one of the greatest tennis players of all time. During her career, she had won a total of thirty-nine Grand Slam career titles. She was also the first female athlete to ever be named *Sports Illustrated* Sportsperson of the Year. In 1971, she hit a major milestone when she became the first female athlete to earn over one hundred thousand dollars in prize money in a single season of competition, but her paycheck was still smaller than the paychecks of her male peers. After winning the US Open in 1972, she threatened to boycott the event going forward if the women's prize money did not match the men's. The US Open gave in, and the following year it became the first major tournament to award equal prize money to men and women.

King became the first president of the Women's Tennis Association in 1973, and her stature as a leader in the feminist movement grew, so when Bobby Riggs (American tennis champion and self-proclaimed "male chauvinist") challenged King to a "Battle of the Sexes," the world paid attention. Riggs claimed that female games were inferior and that he could beat any of the top female players. King agreed to compete against him in a televised match referred to as the "Battle of the Sexes." An estimated ninety million people around the world watched King pulverize Riggs 6–4, 6–3, and 6–3. King made history, proving women were not inferior to men in sports, and in fact, can even be better. The defining moment was later retold in the 2017 movie *Battle of the Sexes*, starring Emma Stone and Steve Carell.

Shortly after the highly publicized match with Riggs, King went on to cofound World Team Tennis, a co-ed league where men and women play a five-set competition in a mix of singles, doubles, and mixed doubles. She also created the Women's Sports Foundation, an organization dedicated to advancing the lives of girls and women through sport and physical activity.

While still married to her husband, King was outed when a palimony lawsuit filed against her by female ex-partner, Marilyn Barnett, became public. She lost major endorsements and faced public backlash because of the affair. King remained married to her husband for a few more years, but they eventually divorced, after she fell in love with her doubles partner, Ilana Kloss. She now lives out and proud.

In 1987, King was inducted into the International Tennis Hall of Fame, and in 2009, she received the Presidential Medal of Freedom for her record of championing human rights, both on and off the court. While there's still a long way to go before we reach full equality, we wouldn't have come this far if it weren't for Billie Jean King.

Esera Tuaolo

NFL Player, Defensive Lineman

"Be welcoming to athletes based on their skills, not based on who they love."

E sera Tuaolo basically lived the American dream. He was born in Hawaii to a family of banana farmers, and grew up in poverty, living with eight brothers and sisters in a dirt-floored hut. He worked hard, graduated college, and went on to have a thriving career in football lasting thirteen years, nine of which were in the NFL.

Tuaolo's talent was recognized early on. He played college football at Oregon State University, and in 1989, he won the Morris Trophy for most outstanding defensive lineman in the league. The Green Bay Packers drafted him the following year, and his professional sports career took off. During his time with the NFL, he played for five teams: the Packers plus the Minnesota Vikings, Jacksonville Jaguars, Atlanta Falcons, and Carolina Panthers. He won the NFC Championship with the Atlanta Falcons and made it all the way to Super Bowl XXXIII, playing against the Denver Broncos.

Even though Tuaolo had a successful career, the stress of being gay and living in the closet took a toll on him. He eventually retired from the NFL, and in 2002, the six-foot-three, three-hundred-pound Samoan football player shattered stereotypes by publicly coming out of the closet on HBO's *Real Sports*. A few years later, he followed up with even more personal details about his life in his autobiography *Alone in the Trenches: My Life As a Gay Man in the NFL*.

Since coming out, Tuaolo has fought for LGBTQ equality and worked on anti-bullying campaigns. He became a board member for the Gay and Lesbian Athletics Foundation and an Advisory Board Member for the You Can Play Project, and he has also worked with the NFL to combat homophobia.

In 2017, Tuaolo stunned the nation once again when he competed on Season Thirteen of *The Voice*, showing everyone that he could sing! While he didn't win the competition, he was able to showcase his stunning vocals, and America welcomed him into their hearts.

Whatever Tuaolo does, it always seems to somehow tie back in to sports. His singing career has led him to perform the National Anthem at sporting events including NFL, MLB, NHL, and NBA games. When he isn't serenading people with his vocal cords, Tuaolo continues to use his voice to speak out for equality. In 2018, he hosted the first annual Inclusion Party at the Super Bowl, benefiting LGBTQ charities in Minneapolis. It was attended by NFL players and various other athletes.

As a gay man with the body of a football player and the voice of an angel, Tuaolo has shown the world that LGBTQ people don't all fit into one small box. We come in all shapes and sizes, and if we work hard and follow our dreams, we can do anything. We can make the world a more inclusive place, and we can even play in the Super Bowl.

Jason Collins

NBA Player, Center

"I think it's important for all of us to celebrate and support everyone to live an authentic life."

Jason Collins always loved basketball, and he was good at it, too. While in high school, he played in two state championships. In college, he played for the Stanford Cardinals, setting a school record for field goal percentage (.608) and ranking all-time third in blocks (89). His NBA career started when he played for the New Jersey Nets in 2001. He wound up making it to nine playoffs during his career, which lasted thirteen NBA seasons.

After the 2012–2013 season ended, Collins made national headlines when he came out as gay. "I'm a thirty-four-year-old NBA center. I'm black. And I'm gay," he wrote in the *Sports Illustrated* cover story. The online version drew 3.7 million unique visitors to the *Sports Illustrated* website. Collins became a free agent, but when he signed a contract with the Nets in 2014, he became the first openly gay active athlete to play in any of the four major US pro sports leagues. Collins chose to wear jersey number 98 in honor of Matthew Shepard, who was murdered in 1998 for being gay. His jersey immediately became the top-selling one at the NBA's online store, and the proceeds were donated to GLSEN and the Matthew Shepard Foundation. In 2014, *Time* magazine featured Collins on their cover and included him on their 100 Most Influential People in the World list.

After that season, Collins retired. He has since dedicated a significant amount of time to charity work, from helping fight childhood obesity to raising money for children of police officers killed on duty. In 2016, he traveled the country to help register people to vote in swing states, and even spoke at the Democratic National Convention.

Collins has secured his place in history and has inspired people around the country both on and off the court.

Stephen Alexander

America's First Openly Transgender Middle School & High School Coach

"Sports are about working with people for a common goal. It's about being part of something larger than yourself."

S tephen Alexander always excelled in sports. During his high school years, he played softball, tennis, basketball, volleyball, and soccer, and collectively, his teams won six state championships. He was well liked by his teammates, and over the course of his high school career, won multiple MVP awards. There was only one problem. All of these achievements were made while playing on girls' teams, and Alexander identified as male.

During college, Alexander came out to his family and began the journey of transitioning. Shortly thereafter, he moved to New York, where he spent time with writers, artists, and activists who also identified as trans/non-binary. After his sister had a baby, Stephen returned home to Rhode Island in order to be the uncle he dreamed he could be.

It wasn't long before Alexander heard about a middle school nearby that needed someone to coach its soccer team. He filled that role and soon found himself coaching the school's basketball, baseball, and tennis teams too. Coaching high school soccer, volleyball, and tennis soon followed.

In 2013, *OutSports* profiled Alexander, calling him "America's First Publicly Out Transgender High School Coach." The story went viral, and Alexander soon saw himself talked about in various news outlets. Nervous at first that there might be a backlash, he was pleasantly surprised when all the coverage seemed to be positive. He was even named one of *Sports Illustrated's* "Trailblazers of the Year" in 2014, and the high school he had attended inducted him into their Athletic Hall of Fame.

In response to all the love and support he received after coming out on the national stage, Alexander became a public speaker, helping schools and organizations better understand issues related to diversity in sports and education. He spends his time promoting inclusivity for all, and stands by his mantra: Everyone Can Play.

Part 10

LITERATURE

Mary Oliver

Pulitzer Prize and National Book Award-Winning Poet

"I've always wanted to write poems and nothing else."

Mary Oliver was born in Maple Heights, Ohio, in 1935 and spent much of her childhood outside, enjoying long walks in nature. She developed an early love of reading, and by the time she was twenty-eight years old had published her first book of poetry, *No Voyage and Other Poems,* in 1963. Now, with well over thirty books in print and a career spanning over half a century, Oliver is widely acknowledged as one of America's most beloved and best-selling poets.

When her sixth book of poetry, *American Primitive,* won the Pulitzer Prize in 1984, everyone asked, "Who's Mary Oliver?" Until then, she had not given even one reading and was leading a quiet life in Provincetown.

Later, she won the prestigious National Book Award for her collection, *New & Selected Poems,* in 1992. Oliver's unique ability to capture the essence of life through poems about animals, plants, the sky, and nature has inspired millions around the world, including Maria Shriver, American journalist and former First Lady of California. Shriver, who interviewed Oliver for *O, The Oprah Magazine* after six years of trying to secure an interview, connected with Oliver's uplifting poetry whose themes of love, survival, gratitude, and joy touch everyone.

One of Oliver's most well-known poems is "The Summer Day," which is often referred to as "The Grasshopper." It ends with the famous and frequently quoted line, "What is it you plan to do with your one wild and precious life?" That one line has radically changed the course of many people's lives, inviting them to look at the bigger picture and decide what's most important to them. Another of Oliver's popular poems is "Wild Geese," which reminds readers that you don't have to be perfect to be alive, you just have to let the animal in you love what it loves.

Even later in her career, Oliver has continued to captivate audiences. At the 2010 California Women's Conference, she shared the stage with other prominent women, including former First Ladies Laura Bush and Michelle Obama, and Supreme Court Justices Ruth Bader Ginsburg and Sandra Day O'Connor. In 2012, readers honored her with the Goodreads Choice Award for Best Poetry.

Many of Oliver's books are dedicated to her partner, photographer and bookstore owner Molly Malone Cook, who died in 2005. Oliver called their relationship a forty-year conversation between artists. Persuaded to move to a warmer climate, Oliver now lives in Florida, and reveals more of her private self in her newer poems. Though she grew up in a "very dark and broken house," she rose above that, saying, "What I have done is learn to love and learn to be loved and that didn't come easy."

Oscar Wilde

Poet, Novelist, and Playwright

"To live is the rarest thing in the world. Most people exist, that is all."

O scar Wilde always dazzled with his words. Born in Dublin in 1854 to a surgeon father and a poet mother, he became one of London's most famous playwrights. More than a hundred years after his death, his plays are among the most widely performed in the English language, and his wit and political satire are just as meaningful today as when they were written.

Best known for his thinly veiled gay novel, *The Picture of Dorian Gray* (1890), universally panned at the time of publication, his first and only novel nonetheless put Wilde at the center of controversy and curiosity. His next years were prolific, bringing *Lady Windemere's Fan* (1892), *A Woman of No Importance* (1893), *An Ideal Husband* (1895) and *The Importance of Being Earnest* (1895), to the forefront of the London stage.

His writings exposed Victorian hypocrisy including social and gender double standards. His work continues to be adapted for stage and film, garnering awards including Golden Globe and Academy Awards. Films and plays based on Wilde or his work have attracted top-tier talent, including Liam Neeson, Julianne Moore, Angela Lansbury, Judi Dench, Stephen Fry, Jude Law, Cate Blanchett, Helen Hunt, Minnie Driver, and others. In 2018, Wilde's short story *The Happy Prince* was made into a film starring Rupert Everett, Colin Firth, Emily Watson. and Tom Wilkinson.

In 1884, Wilde married Constance Lloyd, a wealthy Englishwoman. The couple had two sons, Cyril and Vyvyan, whom Wilde adored. However, in 1893, Wilde became infatuated with Lord Alfred Douglas and the two began a tempestuous affair. When Douglas' father, the Marquess of Queensberry, found out about the affair, he accused Wilde of sodomy, an illegal act at the time. Wilde sued Queensberry for libel, but dropped the lawsuit after it became clear that his private encounters with men would be exposed. But it was too late. The court came to the conclusion that Wilde had broken the law. He was later arrested and charged with "gross indecency." Wilde was convicted and sentenced to two years of hard labor from which, many say, he never recovered. Upon release, he moved to Paris under an assumed name and died in 1900 of meningitis at the age of forty-six. He is buried alongside celebrities in the Père Lachaise Cemetery.

Wilde was a victim of his time, persecuted during his life, but celebrated after his death. Now, many students study Wilde alongside other literary greats such as Charles Dickens, Jane Austen, and Shakespeare. His legacy lives on, inspiring millions of people to be their best selves and not take life too seriously.

Tony Kushner

Award-Winning Playwright and Screenwriter

"The only thing an artist has to do is to try and tell the truth."

Tony Kushner was born in New York City in 1956 to musician parents, but the family moved to Lake Charles, Louisiana, shortly after his birth. His childhood experience of growing up Jewish in the deeply Christian South, in addition to suppressing any conscious awareness of his sexual orientation, significantly influenced his work later in life. The impact of being a minority translated well into his writing and helped spawn one of the most important plays in a generation.

Kushner's play *Angels in America* was a seven-and-a-half-hour, two-day play that went against all the theater conventions of the time. The production was divided into two parts (*Angels in America: Millennium Approaches* and *Angels in America: Perestroika*) and placed a minority group at the center of history. It allowed the American theater-going public to witness a gay storyline as a human one; a story full of love, loss, denial, rejection, survival, intersectionality, and the power of community. It was also one of the first major theatrical works to tackle the subject of AIDS in a way that engaged broad audiences. Kushner won numerous awards for *Angels in America*, including a Pulitzer Prize and two back-to-back Tony Awards, one in 1993 for *Millennium Approaches* and the other in 1994 for *Perestroika*. In 2003, the play was adapted into a miniseries for HBO starring Al Pacino, Meryl Streep, and Emma Thompson. The television version won several Emmy Awards and Golden Globes. The play was revived on Broadway in 2018, with Andrew Garfield and Nathan Lane both winning Tony Awards for their performances.

After *Angels in America* catapulted Kushner into stardom, he went on to write numerous other projects including *Caroline, or Change*, a 2004 musical about a maid and the changes she, and those around her, go through during the American civil rights movement. Kushner took on Hollywood, teaming up with Eric Roth to co-write the award-winning screenplay for Steven Spielberg's 2005 film, *Munich*, starring Eric Bana and Daniel Craig. He later joined Spielberg again on the screenplay for the award-winning 2012 film *Lincoln*, starring Daniel Day-Lewis. *Lincoln* grossed over $275 million at the box office and was nominated for twelve Academy Awards, more than any other film that year.

Kushner is an intellectually robust and prolific writer with the capacity to emotionally connect audiences to historic moments in time. Whether on stage or on screen, his scripts have captivated viewers across the globe. That's why President Obama presented him with the 2012 National Medal of Arts. When it comes to American theater and film, Kushner is an American treasure.

Acknowledgments

We would like to take the opportunity to thank the following people who helped us with this project.

First, and foremost, thank you to our spouses for supporting us through this journey. You were our extra pair of eyes, our cheerleaders, and our therapists. We couldn't have done this without you.

Thank you to Stephen Alexander for helping us with initial proofreading of some of the earlier profiles. Your insight was extremely valuable.

Thank you to our editor, Brenda Knight, for keeping us on track and encouraging us along the way.

Michael Bedwell, thank you for providing feedback on the profile for Leonard P. Matlovich and for keeping his spirit alive through www.leonardmatlovich.com.

Thank you to the entire team at Mango Publishing who helped navigate this project through all phases of production, cover design, editing, formatting, marketing, distribution, and more. You helped make this book a reality and we are forever grateful for your support!

About the Authors

Eric Rosswood is an in-demand authority and commentator on LGBTQ issues including civil rights, parenting, marriage, and politics. He is a major influencer on social media with over 100,000 followers on Twitter alone, and he has led panels on LGBTQ parenting issues for organizations such as the Family Equality Council and the Modern Family Alliance. His bestselling book, Journey to Same-Sex Parenthood, won numerous awards including the best Parenting / Family / Relationships book in the IAN Book of the Year Awards, the best Parenting book in the Readers' Favorite Book Awards, and the best LGBTQ Non-Fiction book in the International Best Book Awards. Rosswood resides in New York with his husband, son, their two cats, and a dog named Mr. Buggles.

Kathleen Archambeau is an award-winning writer and longtime LGBTQ activist. A native San Franciscan, she was a founding contributor to the James Hormel LGBT wing of the San Francisco Public Library. As Vice President and Co-Chair of the Fundraising Committee of the Board of Directors of Operation Concern, one of the oldest and largest mental health agencies serving the LGBT community, she was given an Outstanding Service Award. With her Kiwi wife, Kathleen Archambeau competed and won two Bronze Medals in Ballroom Dancing at the Gay Games in Cologne, Germany. Archambeau contributed a regular column profiling LGBTQ artists in one of the longest-running LGBTQ publications in the US, *The San Francisco Bay Times*. Archambeau's first book, *Climbing the Corporate Ladder in High Heels*, was featured in *Forbes* twice, endorsed by US House of Representatives Majority Leader Nancy Pelosi and CEO and Chair of

BareEssentuals, Leslie Blodgett, and translated into Chinese, Korean, Lithuanian, and Portuguese. Her essay, "Seized," one of only two lesbian creative nonfiction entries in a collection of twenty-one authors entitled, *The Other Woman*, edited by Victoria Zackheim, was lauded by *Publishers Weekly* for its "... top-drawer writers." Kathleen Archambeau was a Department of Education Fellow at the University of Iowa and is a legacy donor focused on LGBTQ writers for the University of Iowa Writers Workshop. She lives with her wife and Guide Dog Career Change Puppy in the San Francisco Bay Area.

Resources

All links active at time of publication.

Introduction

https://ilga.org/downloads/2017/ILGA_State_Sponsored_
Homophobia_2017_WEB.pdf

https://www.counseling.org/news/aca-blogs/aca-government-affairs-blog/
aca-government-affairs-blog/2018/05/31/conversion-therapy-bans-become-
law-in-three-more-states

https://williamsinstitute.law.ucla.edu/press/conversion-therapy-release/

Bayard Rustin

https://obamawhitehouse.archives.gov/the-press-office/2013/11/20/remarks-
president-presidential-medal-freedom-ceremony

https://www.glsen.org/blog/black-history-month-heroes-bayard-rustin

https://www.britannica.com/biography/Bayard-Rustin

https://aflcio.org/about/history/labor-history-people/bayard-rustin

http://www.pbs.org/wnet/african-americans-many-rivers-to-cross/history/100-
amazing-facts/who-designed-the-march-on-washington/

https://www.biography.com/people/bayard-rustin-9467932

https://www.americanprogress.org/issues/lgbt/reports/2013/08/23/72807/
lessons-from-bayard-rustin-why-economic-justice-is-an-lgbt-issue/

https://www.psychologytoday.com/us/blog/the-sexual-continuum/201201/
bayard-rustin-forgotten-civil-rights-hero

https://www.history.com/topics/black-history/march-on-washington

http://www.crmvet.org/docs/moworg2.pdf

https://www.dol.gov/general/aboutdol/hallofhonor/2013_rustin

Emma González

https://www.harpersbazaar.com/culture/politics/a18715714/protesting-nra-gun-control-true-story/

https://www.newyorker.com/news/news-desk/three-days-in-parkland-florida

https://www.washingtonpost.com/news/post-nation/wp/2018/03/01/emma-gonzalez-la-nueva-cara-of-florida-latinx/?utm_term=.336a8bcf3794

https://people.com/crime/parkland-shooting-survivor-emma-gonzalez-more-twitter-followers-nra/

https://www.cnn.com/2018/03/25/us/emma-gonzalez-what-you-need-to-know-trnd/index.html

http://www.foxnews.com/us/2018/02/14/florida-school-shooting-among-10-deadliest-in-modern-us-history.html

https://www.theguardian.com/us-news/ng-interactive/2017/oct/02/america-mass-shootings-gun-violence

https://www.nytimes.com/2018/02/18/us/emma-gonzalez-florida-shooting.html

https://www.cnn.com/2018/03/09/us/florida-gov-scott-gun-bill/index.html

http://www.newsweek.com/march-our-lives-how-many-2-million-90-voting-district-860841

Nyle DiMarco

https://www.gallaudet.edu/news/nyle_dimarco_antm

https://www.washingtonpost.com/lifestyle/style/own-your-identity-the-first-deaf-contestant-on-americas-next-top-model/2015/08/07/6ef1d3b4-39f1-11e5-8e98-115a3cf7d7ae_story.html

https://news.wisc.edu/deaf-actor-activist-nyle-dimarco-connects-with-deaf-students-in-intimate-qa-session/

https://wfdeaf.org/our-work/

https://news.un.org/en/story/2018/09/1019922

https://twitter.com/NyleDiMarco/status/647398826349850624

http://time.com/4301926/dancing-with-the-stars-nyle-dimarco/

https://attitude.co.uk/article/watch-nyle-dimarco-accept-attitudes-man-of-the-year-award-supported-by-virgin-holidays/16108/

Cecelia Maria Zarbo Wambach, PhD

http://ceceliawambach.com/my-life-bio/

https://www.sfgate.com/news/article/Schools-get-1-4-million-from-Hewlett-Annenberg-3138730.php

https://www.linkedin.com/in/wambach-cecelia-85a27245/

https://www.imdb.com/name/nm9048940/

https://refugeeeducationandlearning.org/

https://refugeeeducationandlearning.org/volunteers

https://refugeeeducationandlearning.org/girls-empowerment

https://refugeeeducationandlearning.org/team/

https://www.sfchronicle.com/bayarea/article/East-Bay-retirees-volunteer-in-Greece-with-13001205.php

https://www.sfgate.com/bayarea/article/Bay-Area-educators-reinvent-retirement-on-a-Greek-12980097.php

https://www.unicef.org/eca/press-releases/greece-back-school-refugee-migrant-children

https://www.sfgate.com/opinion/article/EDITORIAL-Teaching-the-Teachers-On-the-job-2850206.php

http://ceceliawambach.com/my-life-bio

Beth Ford

https://www.linkedin.com/feed/update/urn:li:activity:6437698781155770368/

https://www.linkedin.com/pulse/welcome-family-vermont-creamery-beth-ford/

https://www.linkedin.com/pulse/shared-holiday-favorite-beth-ford/

https://www.linkedin.com/pulse/privilege-fulfilling-our-community-commitment-beth-ford/

https://www.linkedin.com/pulse/5-essential-life-hacks-driving-global-business-beth-ford/

https://www.businessinsider.com/beth-ford-land-o-lakes-ceo-2018-7

https://www.landolakesinc.com/Press/News/beth-ford-named-ceo

http://fortune.com/2018/07/26/land-o-lakes-beth-ford-ceo/

https://www.advocate.com/business/2018/7/30/land-olakes-beth-ford-becomes-first-out-woman-run-fortune-500

https://www.bloomberg.com/profiles/people/3598807-beth-e-ford

https://www.huffingtonpost.com/entry/beth-ford-land-olakes-gay-ceo_us_5b5f3004e4b0de86f49966d5

https://www.wsj.com/articles/land-olakes-names-next-ceo-1532611476

http://fortune.com/most-powerful-women/beth-ford-30/

https://www.cnn.com/2018/10/01/business/land-o-lakes-beth-ford/index.html

http://fortune.com/2018/10/02/beth-ford-land-o-lakes/

http://fortune.com/2018/07/26/land-o-lakes-beth-ford-ceo/

https://www.landolakesinc.com/Press/News/beth-ford-named-ceo

http://time.com/money/5409815/land-o-lakes-ceo-beth-ford-career-advice/

https://www.bloomberg.com/research/stocks/private/person.asp?personId=506682

https://www.hrc.org/resources/the-cost-of-the-closet-and-the-rewards-of-inclusion

Rick Welts

https://www.youtube.com/watch?v=e6SR3XyOlqU

https://www.nba.com/warriors/staff/rick-welts

https://www.seattletimes.com/sports/nba/rick-welts-remarkable-journey-from-sonics-ball-boy-to-basketball-hall-of-fame/

https://www.nbcsports.com/bayarea/warriors/rick-welts-hall-fame-personality-deserves-much-praise-anyone

https://abc7news.com/sports/warriors-president-rick-welts-on-being-inducted-to-nba-hall-of-fame/4186486/

https://www.bloomberg.com/research/stocks/private/person.asp?personId=34075339

https://www.symphonicsource.com/blog/11-quotes-on-building-a-championship-culture-from-the-golden-state-warriors/

https://www.sportsbusinessdaily.com/Daily/Issues/1997/10/21/Leagues-Governing-Bodies/BRANDWEEK-HONORS-WNBAS-ACKERMAN-AND-WELTS-AS-TOP-MARKETERS.aspx

http://www.youcanplayproject.org/pages/staff-and-board

http://www.nba.com/video/2018/09/07/20180907-hall-fame-rick-welts-speech

https://www.nba.com/warriors/news/hof-2018-class-announcement-20180331

Suze Orman

https://www.youtube.com/watch?v=GTN9HyOVsUY&feature=youtu.be

https://www.thehotline.org/women-breaking-free

https://www.suzeorman.com/resources

https://www.cnbc.com/video/2018/10/12/suze-orman-you-dont-need-to-buy-a-home-to-be-financially-secure.html

https://www.suzeorman.com/about-suze/tv-radio

https://www.suzeorman.com/products

https://money.cnn.com/2014/11/25/media/new-suze-orman-show/index.html

https://www.businessinsider.com/suze-orman-is-leaving-cnbc-2014-11

http://time.com/money/4989311/retire-like-suze-2/

https://awakenthegreatnesswithin.com/40-inspirational-suze-orman-quotes-on-success/

http://content.time.com/time/specials/2007/article/0,28804,1733748_1733752_1736278,00.html

http://content.time.com/time/specials/packages/
article/0,28804,1984685_1985123_1985086,00.html

https://www.usnews.com/news/blogs/washington-whispers/2008/10/07/suze-
ormans-coming-out-at-the-human-rights-campaign-dinner

https://www.military.com/daily-news/2017/01/04/suze-orman-give-soldiers-
free-money-education-course.html

https://corporate.discovery.com/discovery-newsroom/suze-orman-
at-the-apollo-women-and-money-special-to-air-exclusively-on-own-
monday-october-1/

https://www.hrc.org/blog/video-suze-orman-on-how-doma-hurts-the-
american-economy

https://www.afterellen.com/tv/5276-suze-orman-comes-out-2

https://www.nytimes.com/2007/02/25/magazine/25wwlnq4.t.html

https://people.com/tv/suze-orman-talks-rags-riches-rise-finding-
soulmate-age-50/

Tim Cook

https://www.bloomberg.com/news/articles/2014-10-30/tim-cook-speaks-up

http://time.com/4036006/tim-cook-coming-out-gay/

https://www.cnbc.com/2017/11/06/tim-cooks-performance-as-apple-ceo-
profits-sales-and-innovation.html

https://www.cnbc.com/2015/03/26/apples-tim-cook-will-give-away-
all-his-money.html

https://www.nytimes.com/interactive/2017/12/05/your-money/apple-
market-share.html

https://www.fastcompany.com/3062090/playing-the-long-game-
inside-tim-cooks-apple

https://www.investopedia.com/insights/what-makes-aapl-valuable-company/

https://www.statista.com/statistics/273439/number-of-employees-of-
apple-since-2005/

https://www.inc.com/business-insider/best-quotes-tim-cook.html

http://fortune.com/2017/04/17/apple-ceo-tim-cook-lgbt-free-speech/

https://www.usatoday.com/story/money/2015/03/06/379-companies-want-gay-marriage-bans-overturned/24486461/

https://www.newsweek.com/apple-ceo-tim-cook-shares-tech-giants-plan-fight-racism-after-trumps-651763

https://www.usatoday.com/story/tech/news/2017/02/06/97-tech-firms-file-court-brief-opposing-immigration-ban/97538208/

https://www.wsj.com/articles/workplace-equality-is-good-for-business-1383522254

https://www.telegraph.co.uk/technology/apple/10424816/Apple-CEO-Tim-Cook-speaks-out-for-gay-rights-in-the-workplace.html

https://www.wired.com/2015/07/apple-equality-act/

https://www.wired.com/2015/03/tim-cook-religious-freedom-laws/

https://www.imore.com/history-iphone-original

https://www.usatoday.com/story/money/2018/08/02/apple-first-stock-hit-1-trillion-market-value/877867002/

Bill T. Jones

http://newyorklivearts.org/download/BTJ_FULL_BIO.pdf

https://www.broadwayworld.com/article/2010-Tony-Awards-Bill-T-Jones-Wins-Best-Choreography-20100613

https://www.nytimes.com/2015/06/20/arts/dance/review-bill-t-jones-arnie-zane-summons-a-life-during-wartime.html

https://www.nytimes.com/2007/06/07/arts/dance/07jone.html

http://www.pbs.org/black-culture/shows/list/bill-t-jones-a-good-man/

http://www.pbs.org/wnet/americanmasters/bill-t-jones-a-good-man-biographical-essay-and-tribute/1895/

http://www.kennedy-center.org/artist/A4338

https://www.arts.gov/honors/medals/bill-t-jones

http://content.time.com/time/covers/0,16641,19941010,00.html

https://www.nytimes.com/2016/06/06/t-magazine/bill-t-jones-dance-choreography.html

Jin Xing

https://www.youtube.com/watch?v=IC01XrgzZ7w

http://usa.chinadaily.com.cn/china/2015-10/17/content_22205398.htm

http://www.scmp.com/news/china/society/article/2087720/how-transgender-dancer-jin-xing-conquered-chinese-tv

https://www.pri.org/stories/2015-06-03/10-transgender-icons-around-world-who-should-be-famous-caitlyn-jenner

https://www.hollywoodreporter.com/features/meet-oprah-china-who-happens-be-transgender-942750

https://www.glaad.org/blog/glaad-global-voices-trans-chinese-dancer-does-it-all?response_type=embed

https://www.economist.com/china/2017/02/11/chinas-transgender-oprah

https://www.huffingtonpost.com/2015/04/09/jin-xing-transgender-china_n_7034270.html

https://www.nytimes.com/1999/09/14/world/beijing-journal-as-china-changes-a-sex-change-can-bring-fame.html

https://www.cnn.com/2013/07/11/world/asia/china-jin-xing-sex-change/index.html

https://www.newsweek.com/once-male-soldier-now-female-dancer-china-66057

Daniela Vega

http://remezcla.com/features/film/daniela-vega-a-fantastic-woman/

https://www.theguardian.com/film/2018/mar/01/a-fantastic-woman-review-sebastian-lelio-daniela-vega

https://www.theguardian.com/film/2018/feb/18/daniela-vega-transgender-star-film-industry-a-fantastic-woman-interview

https://www.backstage.com/interview/daniela-vegas-winding-path-acting/

http://time.com/collection-post/5217558/daniela-vega/

http://time.com/collection/most-influential-people-2018/5217558/daniela-vega/

https://www.vice.com/en_us/article/a3795k/an-oscar-nomination-for-daniela-vega-would-make-trans-hollywood-history

https://www.bbc.com/news/world-latin-america-43320379

http://time.com/5186869/daniela-vega-oscars-2018/

http://www.latimes.com/entertainment/movies/la-et-mn-daniela-vega-20171113-htmlstory.html

https://www.wmagazine.com/story/daniela-vega-transgender-actress-oscar-nomination

https://www.harpersbazaar.com/culture/film-tv/a19057004/who-is-daniela-vega-oscars-2018-a-fantastic-woman-nominee/

https://www.nbcnews.com/feature/nbc-out/first-fantastic-woman-wins-oscar-transgender-lead-n853626

https://twitter.com/mbachelet/status/970485105549561856

Ellen DeGeneres

https://www.today.com/popculture/ellen-degeneres-returns-new-orleans-1C9433459

https://www.washingtonpost.com/news/morning-mix/wp/2017/04/28/ellen-made-gay-ok-tv-host-celebrates-20th-anniversary-of-her-coming-out-sitcom-episode/

http://www.pewresearch.org/fact-tank/2013/06/14/ellen-degeneres-is-the-most-visible-gay-or-lesbian-public-figure-in-america/

https://variety.com/2015/tv/news/ellen-degeneres-gay-rights-gay-marriage-1201531462/

https://www.sheknows.com/entertainment/articles/1108319/times-ellen-degeneres-charitable-giving-changed-lives

https://www.youtube.com/watch?v=PWxt-x9Hiql

http://www.foxnews.com/story/2005/09/17/ellen-degeneres-show-pledge-15-million.html

https://www.peta.org/blog/peta-names-man-woman-year/

http://ew.com/article/2016/11/22/ellen-degeneres-presidential-medal-freedom/

https://www.eonline.com/de/news/546034/forbes-100-most-powerful-women-list-revealed-beyonce-ellen-degeneres-and-angelina-jolie-make-the-cut

http://articles.chicagotribune.com/2014-05-29/entertainment/chi-angelina-jolie-oprah-winfrey-beyonce-among-worlds-100-most-powerful-women-20140529_1_angelina-jolie-100-most-powerful-women-first-list

https://www.emmys.com/bios/ellen-degeneres

Robin Roberts

https://www.biography.com/people/robin-roberts-21188247

https://abcnews.go.com/GMA/robin-roberts-biography/story?id=128237

https://rtdna.org/article/rtdnf_announces_2018_first_amendment_award_honorees

http://www.peabodyawards.com/award-profile/robins-journey

https://www.cnn.com/2013/12/29/showbiz/robin-roberts-comes-out

https://abcnews.go.com/GMA/robin-roberts-reports-pass-christian-mississippi-years-hurricane/story?id=11493018

Roberts, *My Story, My Song: Mother-Daughter Reflections on Life and Faith,* Nashville, TN: Upper Room Books, 2012.

Roberts, Robin, *From the Heart: 8 Rules to Live By,* NYC, NY: Hyperion, 2008.

Roberts, Robin, with Veronica Chambers, *Everybody's Got Something*, NYC, NY: Grand Central Publishing, Hachette Book Group, 2014.

https://www.youtube.com/watch?v=vJyCl2uE_cE

https://www.youtube.com/watch?v=7lscELxqihs

https://www.youtube.com/watch?v=AjQf_DBToXA

https://www.youtube.com/watch?v=kQGMTPab9GQ

https://www.youtube.com/watch?v=3TmcB8Bzl38

https://www.youtube.com/watch?v=d0uOoaw21l0

Chris Nee

http://www.peabodyawards.com/award-profile/doc-mcstuffins

https://www.imdb.com/name/nm1349008/awards?ref_=nm_awd

https://variety.com/2015/tv/news/michelle-obama-doc-mcstuffins-1201601593/

https://www.adweek.com/tv-video/disney-wraps-major-upfront-sales-150977/

http://time.com/3079446/disneys-perfect-answer-to-barbie-is-doc-mcstuffins/

https://www.nytimes.com/2014/07/27/business/a-disney-doctor-speaks-of-identity-to-little-girls.html

https://www.workingmother.com/content/chris-nee-disney-junior-doc-mcstuffins

https://www.huffingtonpost.com/author/chris-nee

https://www.glaad.org/blog/how-disney-teaching-valuable-family-lessons-episode-doc-mcstuffins-featuring-wanda-sykes-and

https://www.wired.com/2012/05/doc-mcstuffins-and-writer-producer-chris-nee/

https://thegrio.com/2013/09/30/doc-mcstuffins-creator-explains-why-shows-lead-character-is-black/

Sir Ian McKellen

http://www.bbc.co.uk/bbcthree/article/70b15fcd-3e98-4ce0-a192-5f4b78212ae9

https://www.britannica.com/biography/Ian-McKellen

http://mckellen.com

https://www.stonewall.org.uk/people/ian-mckellen

https://www.biography.com/people/ian-mckellen-9392833

Margaret Cho

https://www.nytimes.com/2014/12/25/us/with-memories-of-a-comic-comrade-margaret-cho-helps-the-homeless.html

https://www.huffingtonpost.com/entry/margaret-cho-bisexuality-pride_us_5b27b980e4b0783ae12b754e

http://news.berkeley.edu/2018/03/22/front-row-with-margaret-cho-and-friends/

https://www.biography.com/people/margaret-cho-20984631

https://www.rollingstone.com/culture/culture-lists/50-best-stand-up-comics-of-all-time-126359/margaret-cho-3-126676/

https://www.npr.org/2011/05/31/136818644/margaret-cho-breaks-barriers-in-world-of-comedy

https://www.fandango.com/people/margaret-cho-116276/biography

https://archives.sfweekly.com/thesnitch/2008/05/01/last-night-margaret-cho-day-at-city-hall

https://www.tvguide.com/celebrities/margaret-cho/bio/163864/

https://www.washingtonpost.com/express/wp/2017/10/13/post-rehab-margaret-cho-has-come-back-to-life-for-her-fresh-off-the-bloat-tour/

http://www.jademagazine.com/Ad_sample_large.html

http://www.pbs.org/wnet/pioneers-of-television/pioneering-people/margaret-cho/

The Wachowskis

https://www.loc.gov/item/prn-12-226/cinematic-firsts-enshrined-in-2012-film-registry/2012-12-19/

https://www.biography.com/people/lana-wachowski-21095557

https://www.biography.com/people/lilly-wachowski-21095529

http://www.imdb.com/title/tt0133093/awards

http://www.imdb.com/name/nm0905154/bio?ref_=nm_ov_bio_sm

https://www.huffingtonpost.com/2012/07/30/matrix-director-sex-change-larry-wachowski_n_1720944.html

http://people.com/movies/lilly-lana-wachowski-how-transgender-siblings-supported-each-other/

Jóhanna Sigurðardóttir

https://www.forbes.com/lists/2009/11/power-women-09_The-100-Most-Powerful-Women_Rank_3.html

http://news.bbc.co.uk/2/hi/europe/7863923.stm

http://www.bbc.com/news/business-11517459

http://www.nordiclabourjournal.org/artikler/portrett/portrait-2012/article.2012-03-07.7696496692

https://www.newstatesman.com/international-politics/2010/01/iceland-interview-economy

https://www.telegraph.co.uk/women/womens-politics/10756847/Icelands-Jonina-Leosdottir-I-was-the-worlds-first-lesbian-First-Lady.html

Leo Varadkar

http://leovaradkar.ie/

https://www.theguardian.com/commentisfree/2017/jun/04/gay-irish-prime-minister-leo-varadkar-fine-gael-taoiseach

https://www.brookings.edu/events/ireland-in-europe-and-the-world-a-conversation-with-irish-taoiseach-leo-varadkar/

https://www.straitstimes.com/world/united-states/irelands-prime-minister-leo-varadkar-defends-undocumented-irish-immigrants

http://www.irishhealth.com/article.html?id=25270

https://www.irishtimes.com/news/politics/varadkar-backs-yes-vote-saying-ireland-should-trust-women-and-trust-doctors-1.3469913

https://www.bbc.com/news/world-europe-40134140

https://www.taoiseach.gov.ie/eng/Taoiseach_and_Government/About_the_Taoiseach/

https://www.britannica.com/biography/Leo-Varadkar

https://www.washingtonpost.com/world/europe/ireland-votes-to-repeal-its-ban-on-abortion/2018/05/26/fb675fa8-603b-11e8-b656-236c6214ef01_story.html

https://www.irishtimes.com/news/social-affairs/why-did-varadkar-change-his-mind-on-abortion-1.3373470

https://www.independent.co.uk/voices/ireland-abortion-referendum-illegal-legal-rape-vote-may-june-2018-20-december-decision-a8110706.html

https://www.bbc.com/news/world-europe-45568094

https://www.nbcnews.com/feature/nbc-out/ireland-appears-set-elect-first-openly-gay-prime-minister-n765426

https://www.theguardian.com/world/2017/jun/02/leo-varadkar-becomes-irelands-prime-minister-elect

https://www.huffingtonpost.com/entry/leo-varadkar-st-patricks-day-parade_us_5aafc8b7e4b0697dfe18b442

https://www.irishtimes.com/news/politics/leo-varadkar-i-am-a-gay-man-minister-says-1.2070189

Eric Fanning

https://www.defense.gov/About/Biographies/Biography-View/article/778714/eric-fanning/

https://www.cbsnews.com/news/a-final-salute-to-eric-fanning/

http://www.washingtonblade.com/2013/04/19/senate-confirms-gay-official-as-air-force-under-secretary/

https://www.washingtontimes.com/news/2016/jun/20/troops-welcome-eric-fanning-army-secretary-with-fa/

https://www.army.mil/article/174964/americas_diversity_is_our_armys_strength

Technical Sergeant Leonard P. Matlovich

http://time.com/4019076/40-years-leonard-matlovich/

http://www.leonardmatlovich.com

https://www.nytimes.com/1988/06/24/us/gay-airman-who-fought-ouster-dies-from-aids.html

https://lgbthistorymonth.com/leonard-matlovich?tab=biography

https://www.airforcetimes.com/news/your-air-force/2015/11/14/on-veterans-day-lgbt-troops-honor-two-of-their-own/

https://www.huffingtonpost.com/jennifer-bendery/leonard-matlovich-gay-veteran_b_6141746.html

Sir Elton John

https://www.biography.com/people/elton-john-9355335

https://www.rollingstone.com/music/artists/elton-john/biography

http://www.guinnessworldrecords.com/world-records/59721-best-selling-single

https://www.billboard.com/articles/columns/chart-beat/5557800/hot-100-55th-anniversary-by-the-numbers-top-100-artists-most-no

https://www.eltonjohn.com/charities

https://www.nytimes.com/2014/11/30/fashion/elton-john-and-darren-walker-on-race-sexual-identity-and-leaving-the-past-behind.html

k.d. lang

https://www.biography.com/people/kd-lang-21174577

https://www.canadaswalkoffame.com/inductees/2008/kd-lang

https://www.grammy.com/grammys/artists/kd-lang

https://www.cbc.ca/news/canada/calgary/kd-lang-fashion-cowboy-bride-coming-out-1.3657007

https://www.nytimes.com/2018/03/22/style/kd-lang-ingenue-tour.html

https://www.washingtonpost.com/archive/lifestyle/1990/07/02/cattle-countrys-beef-with-kd-lang/7dd680b4-ecf0-407a-aed5-b6120b879d38/

https://junoawards.ca/nomination/2013-canadian-music-hall-of-fame-k-d-lang/

http://www.vh1.com/news/1238/the-100-greatest-women-in-music/

https://celebrityaccess.com/caarchive/cmt-reveals-its-list-of-40-greatest-women-in-country-music/

Leonard Bernstein

http://www.classicfm.com/composers/bernstein-l/guides/leonard-bernstein-quotes/

https://leonardbernstein.com/resources/press-room/leonard-bernstein-at-100

https://www.prospectmagazine.co.uk/magazine/leonard-bernstein-invented-how-we-do-modern-classical-music

http://www.interlude.hk/front/leonard-bernstein-felicia-montealegrea-divided-life/

http://www.sfsymphony.org/Watch-Listen-Learn/Read-Program-Notes/Articles-Interviews/My-father-Leonard-Bernstein

http://www.sfsymphony.org/Watch-Listen-Learn/Read-Program-Notes/Articles-Interviews/The-Best-of-All-Possible-Worlds

https://www.biography.com/people/leonard-bernstein-9210269

https://www.britannica.com/biography/Leonard-Bernstein

https://www.npr.org/sections/deceptivecadence/2018/08/25/638625561/life-with-leonard-bernstein

https://nyphil.org/jfk

https://www.whitehousehistory.org/leonard-bernstein-at-the-kennedy-white-house

https://www.loc.gov/item/2010646104/

http://www.praemiumimperiale.org/en/laureate-en/music-en/bernstein-en

http://www.theaterhalloffame.org/members.html#B

https://www.colorado.edu/event/bernstein/leonard-bernstein/accolades

https://www.grammy.com/grammys/artists/leonard-bernstein

Michael Tilson Thomas

http://michaeltilsonthomas.com/2018/01/25/mtt-is-carnegie-hall-perspectives-artist-in-201819-season/

http://michaeltilsonthomas.com/category/photos-videos/

http://gayinfluence.blogspot.com/2011/09/michael-tilson-thomas-american.html

https://www.wsj.com/articles/SB1000142405274870356160457528502480859896

http://worldofwonder.net/bornthisday-conductorcomposer-michael-tilson-thomas/

https://www.youtube.com/watch?v=ujigG6zzbdE

https://www.nws.edu/about/michael-tilson-thomas/

https://www.inspiringquotes.us/author/7790-michael-tilson-thomas/page:2

https://www.nytimes.com/2017/10/31/arts/music/michael-tilson-thomas-san-francisco-symphony.html

https://www.carnegiehall.org/-/media/CarnegieHall/Files/PDFs/About/Press-Resources/2018-2019-Season/1819-Perspectives-Michael-Tilson-Thomas.pdf

https://www.sfsymphony.org/About-Us/Musicians-Conductors/Michael-Tilson-Thomas

https://cso.org/about/performers/conductors/michael-tilson-thomas/

https://www.encyclopedia.com/people/literature-and-arts/music-history-composers-and-performers-biographies/michael-tilson-thomas

https://www.britannica.com/biography/Michael-Tilson-Thomas

https://www.mlive.com/entertainment/index.ssf/2009/04/15m_hits_later_youtube_symphon.html

https://www.arts.gov/honors/medals/michael-tilson-thomas

https://www.sfgate.com/entertainment/article/38-years-together-Tilson-Thomas-and-Robison-marry-5867303.php

https://www.theguardian.com/music/2012/may/25/michael-tilson-thomas-interview

Ricky Martin

https://www.biography.com/people/ricky-martin-9542230

https://www.grammy.com/grammys/artists/ricky-martin

http://www.walkoffame.com/ricky-martin

https://www.unicef.org/people/people_51425.html

https://www.unicef.org/people/people_48227.html

https://people.com/music/ricky-martin-heartbreak-puerto-rico-crisis-i-dont-sleep/

https://www.latintimes.com/ricky-martin-kisses-woman-fan-pays-nearly-100k-lock-lips-singer-was-it-worth-it-380136

Rob Halford

http://www.mtv.com/news/1429870/rob-halford-discusses-sexuality-publicly-for-the-first-time/

https://www.rollingstone.com/t/judas-priest/

https://www.theguardian.com/music/2010/may/20/judas-priest-rob-halford-british-steel

http://teamrock.com/feature/2016-08-02/my-life-story-rob-halford-from-metal-god-to-gay-icon

https://www.grammy.com/grammys/artists/judas-priest

http://www.blabbermouth.net/news/judas-priest-s-rob-halford-i-ve-been-screaming-my-tits-off-for-38-years-now/

https://www.washingtontimes.com/news/2016/oct/13/rob-halford-judas-priest-id-be-dead-without-sobrie/

Archbishop Carl Bean

http://www.sandiegouniontribune.com/sdut-lgbt-foundation-honors-advocates-2015nov05-story.html

https://ufcmlife.org/leadership

https://www.poz.com/article/Carl-Bean-HIV-20150-6208

https://lasentinel.net/carl-bean-i-was-born-this-way.html

http://minorityaidsproject.org/founder/

Bishop V. Gene Robinson

https://www.washingtonpost.com/local/announcing-divorce-gay-bishop-gene-robinson-cites-missed-opportunities/2014/05/05/7c28849c-d485-11e3-aae8-c2d44bd79778_story.html

https://www.youtube.com/watch?v=HqvcPa-BbLc

https://www.youtube.com/watch?v=jIUs4ITbJXo

https://www.episcopalnewsservice.org/2017/05/22/gene-robinson-named-to-two-chautauqua-institution-posts/

https://www.americanprogress.org/issues/religion/news/2010/03/24/7473/get-to-know-bishop-gene-robinson/

https://www.britannica.com/biography/V-Gene-Robinson

http://web.stanford.edu/group/religiouslife/cgi-bin/wordpress/programs/god-believes-in-love/bishop-gene-robinson-biography/

https://www.nytimes.com/2003/11/03/us/openly-gay-man-is-made-a-bishop.html

http://www.pewforum.org/2017/08/08/gay-marriage-around-the-world-2013/

http://www.latimes.com/nation/la-na-boy-scouts-evolution-2017-story.html

https://www.theguardian.com/world/2003/oct/31/gayrights.religion

https://www.telegraph.co.uk/news/worldnews/northamerica/usa/10807887/First-openly-gay-Anglican-bishop-Gene-Robinson-announces-divorce.html

https://www.cbsnews.com/news/gay-bishop-being-honest-04-03-2004/

https://www.nytimes.com/2009/01/13/us/13prayer.html

https://www.salon.com/2007/10/25/film_on_gays/

https://www.metroweekly.com/2007/10/reel-affirmations-100255/

Alan Turing

https://www.britannica.com/biography/Alan-Turing

https://www.biography.com/people/alan-turing-9512017

https://www.forbes.com/sites/daviddisalvo/2012/05/27/how-alan-turing-helped-win-wwii-and-was-thanked-with-criminal-prosecution-for-being-gay/#12061a5f5cc3

https://www.bbc.com/news/technology-18419691

http://www.guinnessworldrecords.com/world-records/highest-death-toll-from-wars/

https://www.history.com/topics/world-war-ii

https://paw.princeton.edu/article/top-25

Dr. Marci Bowers

https://m.youtube.com/watch?v=SM8oL4-xY3k#fauxfullscreen

https://www.youtube.com/watch?v=fdNM2rFfVFY

https://www.huffingtonpost.com/2015/04/01/marci-bowers-gender-reassignment-transgender_n_6980782.html

http://www.latimes.com/world/africa/la-fg-kenya-genital-mutilation-2017-story.html#

https://www.cbsnews.com/news/dr-marci-bowers-on-the-transgender-movement/

https://www.washingtonpost.com/national/health-science/meet-the-gender-affirmation-surgeon-whose-waiting-list-is-three-years-long/2016/04/22/a4019f2e-f690-11e5-8b23-538270a1ca31_story.html

http://www.who.int/news-room/fact-sheets/detail/female-genital-mutilation

https://www.unicef.org/media/files/FGMC_2016_brochure_final_UNICEF_SPREAD.pdf

Sally Ride, Ph.D.

https://www.nasa.gov/sites/default/files/atoms/files/ride_sally.pdf

https://www.space.com/16756-sally-ride-biography.html

https://www.space.com/40916-sally-ride-pride-inspiration-legacy.html

https://www.history.com/news/navy-christens-research-ship-named-for-sally-ride

https://www.history.com/news/sally-ride-first-astronaut-sexism

https://www.nasa.gov/audience/forstudents/k-4/stories/nasa-knows/who-was-sally-ride-k4.html

https://www.biography.com/people/sally-ride-9458284

https://airandspace.si.edu/collection-objects/award-ncaa-silver-anniversary-student-athlete-sally-ride

Abby Wambach

Forward: A Memoir, Abby Wambach, Harper-Collins, New York: 2016. Paperback: 2017.

http://fortune.com/2016/04/22/us-soccer-abby-wambach-pay/

https://www.youtube.com/watch?v=cAGlK9Vrqel

https://www.ussoccer.com/womens-national-team/thanks-abby/151214-abby-wambach-family-testimonials

https://www.ussoccer.com/stories/2015/10/27/18/45/151027-wnt-abby-wambach-announces-retirement

http://time.com/5281711/abby-wambach-barnard-commencement-2018-speech/

https://www.nytimes.com/2011/07/17/sports/soccer/womens-world-cup-abby-wambach-stands-tall-for-us.html?pagewanted=all

https://floridagators.com/news/2012/4/5/22844.aspx

http://time.com/3823298/abby-wambach-2015-time-100/

https://www.eonline.com/news/779476/espy-awards-2016-winners-the-complete-list

https://www.npr.org/sections/thetwo-way/2015/10/27/452260571/obama-to-u-s-womens-soccer-team-playing-like-a-girl-means-youre-a-badass

https://www.nytimes.com/2008/07/17/sports/olympics/17abby.html

https://www.fifa.com/womens-football/news/y=2015/m=12/news=abby-wambach-ten-defining-moments-2745327.html

http://fortune.com/2015/12/18/abby-wambach-earnings/

Billie Jean King

http://parentingaces.com/hbo-sports-billie-jean-king-portrait-pioneer/

https://www.amazon.com/Pressure-Privilege-Lessons-Learned-Library/dp/0981636802

https://www.youtube.com/watch?v=QUPI5HLLojg

https://www.youtube.com/watch?v=MyMtOwwtJW0

https://www.amazon.com/American-Masters-Billie-Jean-King/dp/B00JUIZTMM

https://www.biography.com/people/billie-jean-king-9364876

https://www.nytimes.com/2006/04/26/arts/television/the-legacy-of-billie-jean-king-an-athlete-who-demanded.html

https://www.espn.com/sportscentury/features/00016060.html

https://www.cnn.com/2014/02/24/sport/tennis/billie-jean-king-fast-facts/index.html

https://www.nbcnews.com/feature/nbc-out/it-was-horrible-billie-jean-king-recalls-being-publicly-outed-n804451

https://www.encyclopedia.com/people/sports-and-games/sports-biographies/billie-jean-king

https://www.history.com/topics/womens-history/billie-jean-king

https://www.britannica.com/biography/Billie-Jean-King

http://www.pbs.org/wnet/americanmasters/billie-jean-king-filmmaker-essay-on-billie-jean-king/2714/

http://www.nydailynews.com/sports/more-sports/billie-jean-king-confesses-1981-lesbian-article-1.2615020

https://www.si.com/sports-man/2010/11/30/billiejeanking-sportsman

https://www.si.com/si-sportsperson-history-female-winners-serena-williams

https://www.theguardian.com/world/2017/nov/12/billie-jean-king-tennis-equality-battle-of-the-sexes

https://www.phillymag.com/articles/2011/06/17/billie-jean-king-racquet-revolutionary/4/

https://www.usopen.org/en_US/news/articles/2018-08-21/50_moments_that_mattered_us_open_is_first_grand_slam_tournament_to_offer_equal_prize_money.html

https://obamawhitehouse.archives.gov/blog/2009/07/30/presidential-medal-freedom-recipients

Esera Tuaolo

http://eseratuaolo.me/biography/

https://www.glaad.org/blog/esera-tuaolo-explains-why-he-hopes-his-first-ever-super-bowl-inclusion-party-will-change-game-lgbtq-professional-sports

https://people.com/archive/gay-man-in-the-nfl-vol-65-no-9/

https://www.today.com/popculture/former-nfl-player-esera-tuaolo-wows-judges-voice-song-story-t116706

http://morristrophy.com/past-winners/players/esera-tuaolo/

https://abcnews.go.com/GMA/story?id=125632&page=1

https://www.nbc.com/the-voice/credits/credit/season-13/esera-tuaolo

https://www.npr.org/templates/story/story.php?storyId=5190140

https://www.nytimes.com/2002/10/27/sports/backtalk-toughest-play-for-veteran-of-nfl-trench-warfare.html

https://today.oregonstate.edu/archives/2003/may/osu-alum-tuaolo-speak-osu-about-nfl-life-gay-athlete

http://a.espncdn.com/nfl/news/2002/1024/1450380.html

https://www.outsports.com/2018/2/2/16962980/super-bowl-52-lgbt-inclusion-party-esera-tuaolo

Jason Collins

http://webtv.un.org/www.unwomen.org/en/executive-board/watch/martina-navratilova-and-jason-collins-on-sport-and-the-fight-against-homophobia-press-conference/2919746360001/

http://lapmf.org/events/golf-tournament/

http://www.lapdonline.org/november_2016/news_view/61440

https://www.prnewswire.com/news-releases/heroes-for-heroes-3rd-annual-los-angeles-police-memorial-foundation-celebrity-poker-tournament--casino-night-party-300513993.html

http://time.com/70898/jason-collins-2014-time-100/

https://www.si.com/more-sports/2013/04/29/jason-collins-gay-nba-player

https://www.si.com/more-sports/2013/04/29/jason-collins-reveals-gay-nba-story

https://www.bbc.com/news/world-us-canada-22341153

https://mashable.com/2013/04/30/jason-collins-sports-illustrated-traffic/

https://www.nytimes.com/2014/03/03/sports/basketball/jason-collins-brooklyn-debut-recalls-jackie-robinsons-in-1947.html

https://pac-12.com/article/2001/05/07/stanfords-jason-collins-declares-nba-draft

https://www.buzzfeed.com/driadonnaroland/nba-will-donate-sales-of-jason-collins-jersey-to-lgbt-groups

https://www.si.com/nba/2016/11/01/jason-collins-hillary-clinton-election-campaign-trail

https://www.healthiergeneration.org/articles/chelsea-clinton-jillian-michaels-and-leading-health-advocates-honor-the-nations-healthiest

Stephen Alexander

https://www.outsports.com/2013/11/12/5095154/transgender-coach-stephen-alexander-profile-glocester-rhode-island

https://www.youtube.com/watch?v=NMTE1o1zLFk

https://www.si.com/vault/issue/1012641/147

http://turnto10.com/archive/only-on-10-transgendered-coach-works-at-ponagnaset-high-school

https://qsaltlake.com/news/2017/03/06/stephen-alexander-little-rhodys-big-trans-man/

http://www.valleybreeze.com/2014-08-13/observer-smithfield-west/ponaganset-hall-fame-induction-dinner-sept-27#.W1HpeLHMxE4

https://fosterponaganseths.ss11.sharpschool.com/athletics/athletic_hall_of_fame

http://www.glocesterri.org/2015Minutes.pdf

https://competenetwork.com/faces-of-sports-transgender-athlete-stephen-alexander/

https://boston.edgemedianetwork.com/news/national/152684/rhode_island_home_to_1st_transgender_high_school_coach

http://www.transyouthequality.org/about-us/

https://www.huffingtonpost.com/grace-anne-stevens/my-transgender-life-where_b_7633434.html

Mary Oliver

http://www.oprah.com/entertainment/Maria-Shriver-Interviews-Poet-Mary-Oliver

https://vimeo.com/236014103

https://www.newyorker.com/magazine/2017/11/27/what-mary-olivers-critics-dont-understand

http://blindflaneur.com/2010/08/19/mary-oliver-%E2%80%98a-bride-married-to-amazement%E2%80%99/

http://www.grolierpoetrybookshop.org/HallofFamep7.html

https://www.poetryfoundation.org/poets/mary-oliver

http://maryoliver.beacon.org/

https://www.goodreads.com/book/show/178959.American_Primitive

https://artsandletters.org/academy-members/

https://www.pulitzer.org/winners/mary-oliver

https://www.britannica.com/biography/Mary-Oliver

https://www.poets.org/poetsorg/poet/mary-oliver

https://www.goodreads.com/choiceawards/best-poetry-books-2012

http://mariashriver.com/mystory/first-lady-of-california/

https://www.independent.co.uk/news/obituaries/molly-malone-cook-310749.html

http://www.nationalbook.org/people/mary-oliver/

Oscar Wilde

https://www.nytimes.com/1998/03/26/theater/arts-abroad-the-ideal-martyr-oscar-wilde-has-the-last-laugh.html

https://www.washingtonpost.com/blogs/answer-sheet/post/irish-authors-the-10-most-read/2012/03/09/gIQAheLIDS_blog.html

http://www.dramaonlinelibrary.com/playwrights/oscar-wilde-iid-12322?start=0

https://www.biography.com/people/oscar-wilde-9531078

https://www.theguardian.com/books/2003/may/07/top10s.oscar.wilde

https://www.youtube.com/watch?v=cqRwZz7n8o8

Tony Kushner

https://www.nytimes.com/2017/09/07/theater/angels-in-america-is-returning-to-broadway-with-nathan-lane.html

http://www.imdb.com/name/nm1065785/bio?ref_=nm_ov_bio_sm

https://www.nytimes.com/2018/03/07/theater/tony-kushner-angels-in-america-broadway.html

http://time.com/5165784/angels-in-america-original-reviews/

http://variety.com/2018/legit/news/original-angels-in-america-ambitious-theater-1202706599/

https://www.britannica.com/biography/Tony-Kushner

https://study.com/academy/lesson/tony-kushner-biography-plays.html

https://www.encyclopedia.com/people/literature-and-arts/theater-biographies/tony-kushner

https://www.pulitzer.org/winners/tony-kushner

https://www.boxofficemojo.com/movies/?id=lincoln.htm

https://www.arts.gov/honors/medals/tony-kushner

https://www.oscars.org/oscars/ceremonies/2013

https://www.imdb.com/event/ev0000383/2005/1

Photo Credits

pg.16 (Bayard Rustin): Shutterstock/AP/Jacob Harris

pg.19 (Emma González): Shutterstock/lev radin

pg.22 (Nyle DiMarco): Shutterstock/DFree

pg.25 (Cecelia Maria Zarbo Wambach, PhD): Bobbi Ausubel

pg.29 (Beth Ford): GettyImages/Stringer/Phillip Faraone

pg.32 (Rick Welts): GettyImages/Staff/Maddie Meyer

pg.35 (Suze Orman): Shutterstock/s_bukley

pg.37 (Tim Cook): Shutterstock/Laura Hutton

pg.42 (Bill T. Jones): Shutterstock/BEI/Carolyn Contino

pg.45 (Jin Xing): Shutterstock/Jonathan Browning

pg.49 (Daniela Vega): Shutterstock/Cineberg

pg.52 (Ellen DeGeneres): Shutterstock/Kathy Hutchins

pg.55 (Robin Roberts): Shutterstock/Leonard Zhukovsky

pg.58 (Chris Nee): Shutterstock/AP/Invision/Charles Sykes

pg.61 (Sir Ian McKellen): Shutterstock/magicinfoto

pg.63 (Margaret Cho): Shutterstock/s_bukley

pg.66 (The Wachowskis): Shutterstock/Variety/David Buchan and Shutterstock/DFree

pg.69 (Jóhanna Sigurðardóttir): GettyImages/Contributor/ullstein bild

pg.72 (Leo Varadkar): Shutterstock/Alexandros Michailidis

pg.75 (Eric Fanning): Shutterstock/Epa/Shawn Thew

pg.78 (Technical Sergeant Leonard P. Matlovich): Brandon Wolf

pg.82 (Sir Elton John): Shutterstock/Featureflash Photo Agency

pg.85 (K.D. Lang): Shutterstock/s_bukley

pg.88 (Leonard Bernstein): Shutterstock/AP/Anonymous

pg.91 (Michael Tilson Thomas): Shutterstock/AP/Lynne Sladky

pg.94 (Ricky Martin): Shutterstock/DFree

pg.97 (Rob Halford): Shutterstock/Northfoto

pg.101 (Archbishop Carl Bean): GettyImages/Contributor/ Carlos Chavez

pg.104 (Bishop V. Gene Robinson): Shutterstock/EPA/C.j. Gunther

pg.108 (Alan Turing): Wikipedia/Public Domain/Anonymous

pg.111 (Dr. Marci Bowers): Shutterstock/lev radin

pg.114 (Sally Ride, PhD): Shutterstock/mark reinstein

pg.118 (Abby Wambach): Shutterstock/AP/Gerald Herbert

pg.121 (Billie Jean King): Shutterstock/Krista Kennell

pg.124 (Esera Tuaolo): Shutterstock/BEI/Matt Baron

pg.127 (Jason Collins): Shutterstock/s_bukley

pg.130 (Stephen Alexander): Eric Rosswood

pg.134 (Mary Oliver): Shutterstock/AP/MARK LENNIHAN

pg.137 (Oscar Wilde): Shutterstock/Everett Historical

pg.140 (Tony Kushner): Shutterstock/Ga Fullner